Praise for *No Regrets*

"Incredible! Dr. Howatt offers the tools you need to live a fulfilled life with peace, leaving shame, regret, and questions of 'what if' behind. Insightful and relevant like never before!"

DR. MARSHALL GOLDSMITH, Thinkers50 #1 Executive Coach; *New York Times*—bestselling author, *The Earned Life, Triggers,* and *What Got You Here Won't Get You There*

"Dr. Bill Howatt has assembled a brilliant and practical guide to navigating and overcoming regret and its accompanying sense of overwhelm. Grounded in science but also personal and inspirational, *No Regrets* will help you move forward in a challenging world regardless of what has happened in your life up until this point."

GREG WELLS, PhD, author, *The Ripple Effect*

"Dr. Bill Howatt's book *No Regrets* takes you on a deep and powerful journey on the importance of simply letting go of any regrets in business and life! The lessons we can learn from regretful experiences are invaluable! This book will take you on a path of being grateful, positive, and most importantly, self-love!"

JOHN "GUCCI" FOLEY, bestselling author, *Fearless Success*

"*No Regrets* provides a timely roadmap to emotional well-being by equipping readers to tame their fears, overcome past regrets, and shift from mindset of surviving to thriving."

MICHEL RODRIGUE, president and CEO, Mental Health Commission of Canada

"*No Regrets* is one of those books that meets you regardless of your stage of life."

DAVE VEALE, founder and CEO, Vision Coaching Inc.

"Two words come to mind when I think about how to apply the wisdom in this book... deliberate and intentional. Dr. Howatt always provides relatable teachings and practical tools for moving forward in a positive direction with our emotional well-being!"

LYNN BROWNELL, CEO, WSPS

"Dr. Howatt's *No Regrets* provides the ingredients I didn't know I needed to solve a problem I didn't know I needed to solve. I now have the tools to live regret-free."

ERIC TERMUENDE, co-founder, NoW of Work

"Dr. Howatt is helping us improve the quality of our lives by moving toward what serves us and away from what does not."

MARY ANN BAYNTON, CEO of Mary Ann Baynton & Associates Corp.

"In his new book, *No Regrets*, Bill lays out a perspicuous path to an increasingly elusive condition: peace of mind. Who doesn't want that?"

KELLY VANBUSKIRK, QC, PhD, C.Arb., lawyer and partner, Lawson Creamer

"In a post-COVID-19 world, when everyone is having regrets, this book is timely. Discover your personal journey with *No Regrets*."

ELAINE CHIN, MD, MBA, founder, Innovation Health Group and Executive Health Centre

"Dr. Bill Howatt offers a much-needed reckoning to our understanding of regret. This refreshing, research-informed, and practical book offers relevant tools to loosen the regret grip. This work is going to change lives by showing how to finally let go, so we can hold tight to brighter futures."

DR. ROBYNE HANLEY-DAFOE, author, *Calm within the Storm*

NO REGRETS

NO REGRETS

Dr. Bill Howatt

HOW TO LIVE TODAY FOR TOMORROW'S EMOTIONAL WELL-BEING

●● PAGE TWO

Cataloguing in publication information is available from Library and Archives Canada.

ISBN 978-1-77458-183-4 (paperback)
ISBN 978-1-77458-184-1 (ebook)

Page Two
pagetwo.com

Edited by Al Kingsbury, Amanda Lewis, and Emily Schultz
Copyedited by Jenny Govier
Cover design by Taysia Louie
Interior design and illustrations by Taysia Louie
Printed and bound in Canada by Friesens
Distributed in Canada by Raincoast Books
Distributed in the US and internationally by Macmillan

22 23 24 25 26 5 4 3 2 1

billhowatt.com

*To all my mentors—and there have been many—
from elementary school, junior and senior high school,
university, and graduate school, to my first job at
the Nova Scotia Youth Centre, to my days on Wall Street.
I can look back at a moment when I was filled with
regret and recall each mentor who guided me to believe
in what is possible, not what had happened or what
I had not tried.*

*Living a life with no regrets is impossible. However,
when we are open to doing the work, we can learn from
regret that can be transformational. My mentors have
inspired me to write this book to provide a path for learning
from regret rather than fearing it, to provide tools for
managing it rather than getting stuck in it, and to help
others not only live with it but thrive by moving toward
the life they really want.*

Contents

Introduction

I S YOUR life going the way you want it to? Beyond yes or no, one way to explore this question is to write your obituary. Based on your current track, what would you feel comfortable writing?

When I suggest this exercise to a client, I notice more often than not the person will pause and say, "I'm not sure what I would write." My response: "That's fine. Would you want to report that you lived a meaningful life with no major regrets?" Most answer, "Yes."

Many of us are racing through each day, week, and month, trying to keep up with the demands of life. With this comes distraction and the risk of missing the gift of each day. A person facing death who believes they lived a meaningful life with no regrets has more peace of mind than one filled with regret and struggling to find meaning.

I've never met the Dalai Lama, but I am a fan. Finding inner peace is one of my favourite insights from him. It comes down to discovering how to become content with where we are and what we have. His point is that waiting for more is unnecessary because we have all we need now to be content, which some may call happy, provided we can learn to manage our unpleasant thoughts and emotions instead of letting them control us. Managing thoughts and emotions is achievable for many, even those who don't believe it is.

We hear so many tragic stories every day, but not being directly involved, most of us never fully comprehend their significance. Consider Jonathan, who on his way home from an average day at work was hit by a transfer truck. He's now paralyzed from the neck down and will never be able to play catch with his son again.

As Jonathan was lying in his hospital bed, his level of regret spiked higher and higher, and with this came increased levels of other unpleasant emotions. For weeks before the accident, his son had been asking him to play catch. He had rationalized that he would do it another day, as work was more important than playing for five minutes with his son. Jonathan realized he had taken his tomorrows for granted. When we're present in our life, we're aware of today's decisions and choices and their impact on our future.

Most of us could not imagine the hardship Jonathan went through physically, cognitively, and emotionally. I've seen firsthand how a tragic outcome shifts perspective and priorities. Jonathan eventually learned how to have different kinds of play with his son. He first needed to move past his regret and look for new opportunities. He concluded that he could be a present father as long as he and his son were together.

Regret is powerful enough to make our emotions spiral out of control, but it also may be the most powerful emotion for prompting us to take action and transform our lives. One research study suggested that regret was valued above all other unpleasant emotions for its potential for personal growth and change.[1] The opportunity for transformational growth from regret comes when our mental state is open to accepting that we can learn to create better outcomes and that it's okay to try.[2]

Why I Wrote This Book

While this book's title may make it appear that it's focused only on regret, it has a much broader utility. It's designed so that you can apply its content to manage any unpleasant emotion better. Getting stuck in an unpleasant emotion such as anger, shame, guilt, or worry for an extended period increases the risk of emotional upset that can lead to regret. Emotional well-being can be defined by the degree you believe you can navigate your current situation, including any unpleasant emotions and thoughts that arise. Notice I didn't say stop these emotions and thoughts. It's not realistic to think that life will be perfect, with no potholes. The good news is we're learning machines and can acquire new knowledge and skills to move past many of life's potholes.

Stephen Covey's *The 7 Habits of Highly Effective People* is an excellent tool for improving emotional well-being.[3] Covey suggests that we can't change things outside our circle of control, only how we respond to them. He purports that we can only directly control our behaviours and choices. We have a choice as to how we respond to any life event. Many react by becoming upset, which strains their emotional well-being.

We all face the task of navigating unpleasant emotions. It typically makes things worse when we try to avoid dealing with situations to which we've attached these emotions. Failure to deal with unpleasant emotions like regret can erode mental health and result in mental illness like depression. We have a global human crisis in coping with unpleasant emotions. I believe that the inability to deal with emotions related to addiction, violence, and suicide contributes to a global increase in mental illness. Data from the World Health Organization indicates that, based on current predictions, depression will be the leading cause of disease globally by 2030.[4] This prediction was made before COVID-19. There's more than enough evidence now that emotional well-being must become a priority.

In our day-to-day experiences, our emotional well-being can become strained, and we can move into a feeling of languishing (e.g., feeling blah), such as not being satisfied with our current job. What can hold some of us back from acting may be fear. In my book *Stop Hiding and Start Living*, I provide an *F*-it model designed to help you move from fear to flourishing.[5] Staying in a job that is not meaningful can one day become a regret.

Another factor that can affect our emotional well-being is feeling isolated and alone. The absence of authentic connections can have a negative impact on our mental health. A study reported in the *Lancet* in 2020 indicated why employers must pay attention to isolation and loneliness. Regarding "the workers assigned periods of perceived isolation," it found that even a period of under ten days can have long-term effects, with the presence—up to three years later—of psychiatric symptoms.[6] In my previous book, *The Cure for Loneliness: How to Feel Connected and Escape Isolation*, I provide a model for building meaningful social connections with self and others.[7] We humans need authentic connections for good mental health. When we do not learn how to develop meaningful, authentic connections, we can get trapped in regret.

There are two types of regret I'll explore in this book:

- In the first type, something happens in our lives, and we have regret about how we reacted and what we did.

- In the second type, we regret what *didn't* happen: that we did not take a chance and try. Often this is the harder form of regret to work through.

Sometimes our regret is immediate, as when we have a loss or a breakup. We might feel that regret instantly and acutely.

In other cases, we may not feel our regret right away (anger may come first). It may take several weeks for what has happened to sink in. Either way, understanding regret and how to move beyond it is important.

Your mental health will not be fixed just by reading a book, taking a course, using an app, or following an employer's initiative. Any kind of transformation requires learning, action, and developing news habits. You know that if you pay attention to your physical health with exercise, diet, rest, and lifestyle choices, you reduce your risk of chronic disease. It's up to you to pull the physical health behaviour levers. Many people are not clear on what levers (i.e., things within their control) they can pull to improve their emotional well-being. Each chapter in Part B of this book contributes to an ingredient that can be used as a lever to move past unpleasant emotions like regret.

REFLECTION

Take a moment and reflect on where you are today and where you think you will land in your lifetime. Be curious without judgement and reflect on your truth.

- Write the first paragraph of your obituary. Describe how you want to be remembered: "[Name] was a..."

- It's okay if you're not ready or sure what to write now. Consider setting a goal within the next thirty days to go beyond the first paragraph and write your full obituary. Then, look at where you are now to determine what opportunities you have to make changes that will help you land where you want to be in this lifetime.

We'll never get back this day or this moment. Too many of us are not awake or aware, do not appreciate how wonderful this moment can be, and are not open to the possibility that it could be the best moment up to this point in our life. We live in the moment, never in the past or the future. Time passes at a constant rate, and our time on this planet is finite. The American Time Use Survey provides a humbling insight into how the average employed person spends each day:[8]

- 9.19 hours on personal care, including sleep
- 6.27 hours working and on work-related activities (average employed full time)
- 1.43 hours on household activities
- 1.16 hours eating and drinking
- 1.20 hours caring for others in and out of the home
- 4.01 hours on leisure and sports

To take charge of emotional well-being requires paying attention first and becoming aware of space and opportunity to invest time into self-care. Do you feel like you're living on a treadmill? Busy lives and intentional lives are not the same. How we perceive our life influences our mood and emotional well-being.

Emotional well-being is the subjective experience we have each day. Our confidence in meeting the demands of life, feeling comfortable, and managing our emotions and thoughts defines our emotional well-being, which is perceived to be in a desirable state when we spend more time than not thinking we're flourishing. We'll never be flourishing 100 percent of the time; however, flourishing 70 percent is much more fulfilling than 30 percent.

Flourishing is more than being happy. Dr. Martin Seligman suggests that flourishing results from building and maintaining the five aspects of the PERMA model: positive emotion, engagement (e.g., work and community), relationships, meaning (e.g., purpose in life), and accomplishments.[9] Dr. Lynn Soots describes flourishing as "the product of the pursuit and engagement of an authentic life that brings inner joy and happiness through meeting goals, being connected with life passions, and relishing in accomplishments through the peaks and valleys of life."[10] Flourishing is the result of making decisions and focusing with intention. It has nothing to do with luck.

This book is for adults who want to learn how to spend more time flourishing and less energy and time experiencing unpleasant emotions like regret.

Five Ingredients for Living with No Regrets

Each section of Part B focuses on one of the five ingredients of a life lived with no regrets: realization, realignment, reputation, reserves, and reset (Figure 1). Each chapter provides you with insights and learnings that make up those ingredients. The five ingredients are designed to help you develop your emotional well-being by teaching you how to spend less time in unpleasant emotions. They are *ingredients* rather than *steps* because they don't need to be done in order, and you may use more of one than another. It really depends on you and the nourishment you need at this time. With the ingredients, you will prepare a personalized recipe for increased emotional well-being.

One key to living with no regrets and feeling you're living your life with meaning is having more pleasant emotions and fewer unpleasant emotions. You don't have to be trapped in unpleasant emotions and negative thoughts most of the time. There's no escaping them, and as you'll discover in Chapter 1, they do serve a purpose, but if you could learn to spend your life with, for example, 80 percent pleasant and 20 percent unpleasant emotions, you would enjoy a higher degree of emotional well-being and mental health than someone who spends 80 percent in unpleasant emotions and 20 percent in pleasant. You can learn to better manage your emotional well-being provided you value it and want your time to be more pleasant than unpleasant. However, there is no shortcut to learning how to reduce the time you spend in unpleasant emotions like regret. Emotional well-being is not intuitive; it requires personal insights, intention, and a willingness to learn to manage your emotions and thoughts better. Doing so requires practising with intention, and it requires patience, as this process can take time and focus. But you have only one life to live, and your decisions form that life.

How to Benefit the Most from This Book

There's no goal line to emotional well-being. It's all about discovering how we can enjoy our pleasant moments and not allow unpleasant ones to control us. Thoughts won't make change; only actions will. I've created this book to be an emotional well-being resource, leveraging a cognitive-behavioural approach for managing unpleasant emotions. Through practice and self-discipline, you'll learn how to master the ideas and skills presented. Think of this book as a short course in emotional well-being. What I will suggest is not complex, nor is it hard to learn. It's practical information that requires intention, time, and patience.

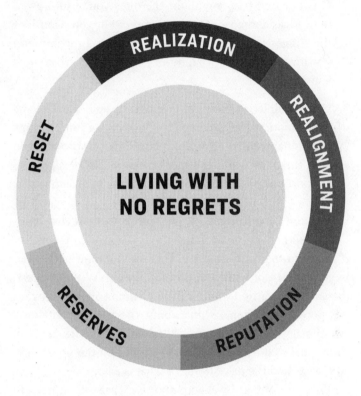

FIGURE 1. THE FIVE INGREDIENTS.

I suggest the following game plan for using this book with intention:

- Read the book for an introduction to the five ingredients. There are different challenges and suggestions for action. On your first pass, highlight the ones you're interested in or ideas and concepts that jump out at you. Consider the suggestions and activities as options. I recommend waiting until the last chapter before deciding what you'll commit to doing.

- Upon completing the book, leverage the epilogue, "Baking Your Emotional Well-Being Plan," and create your monthly emotional well-being action plan. This can provide you with the framework for a mental fitness plan designed to support your ability to cope with unpleasant emotions.

You can have a profound, positive impact on your emotional well-being by making it a priority. It's no different than if you want to become more effective as a parent or partner, in your career, or with your physical fitness. Without effort, focus, and attention, there's little chance you'll reach your full potential. When I think about the road to obtaining emotional well-being, the word "relentless" comes to mind. Emotional well-being is a moving target that requires intensity, pace, and the drive to reject what is easy.

I'm grateful that I wake up knowing that I don't need to fear unpleasant emotions and thoughts. I can't control them; I can only manage them. I share this because even mental health experts are challenged every day to believe things will be okay. My mental fitness plan is the saviour of my emotional well-being. It consists of the things I do daily to support and promote pleasant emotions. As you go through this book, you will be exposed to microskills you can practise and add to daily routines that help you focus on what you can control. In the last chapter of the book, you will be encouraged to develop a plan to support your emotional well-being.

The end goal for emotional well-being is not an event; it's a lifelong pursuit, no different than maintaining physical health. If you want to be physically healthy, you must learn to push yourself and make hard choices, such as exercising and eating a healthy, balanced diet versus the easy choice of doing nothing more than sitting on the couch in front of the TV. Emotional well-being is the same; it doesn't happen randomly. It happens when we make it a priority and do the work required to make it so. The long-term benefits are increased contentment, happiness, and fulfillment—the holy grail of the human experience. If you're open to this possibility, you may discover in a relatively short time that you can learn to have all you need to experience happiness from within.

PART A

DISCOVERING WHAT REGRET IS AND WHY IT HURTS

**Forget regret,
or life is yours to miss.**

JONATHAN LARSON

THIS PART of the book digs into what the word "regret" means emotionally and how it can—if not managed and dealt with—alter your perception of your life. The following key topics will be covered in Part A:

- The types of regret
- The degree to which regret influences emotional well-being
- The link between regret and other unpleasant emotions
- How a person can get stuck in regret
- The benefits of regret

What Is Regret?

ASSUMING EVERYONE has a clear frame of reference for regret would be a mistake. Did you know before reading the introduction to this book that regret is perhaps the most powerful unpleasant emotion for facilitating emotional transformation? To navigate this emotion, it's important to know not only what regret is but also how it may be inhibiting your emotional well-being. We all experience moments of regret because we make mistakes. It's not the mistakes that matter so much as what we do when we make them.

An important distinction is between living with regret and having regret. Living with regret means it's constantly affecting your emotional well-being. Having regret is an opportunity to learn from a mistake or to summon the courage to act so you don't miss out on an opportunity that could have a positive impact on you at some level, such as an experience that will influence a career or lifestyle choice.

Most of us understand regret at a surface level. However, I suspect few truly understand the value and benefits of this

emotion. Every unpleasant emotion has an evolutionary purpose, but without insight at the moment it's experienced,
it's seldom viewed as an opportunity. The ultimate purpose
of all unpleasant emotions is to help us survive. As much as
we may not want to experience unpleasant emotions, their
role is to move us toward and away from certain situations for
self-protection. Pick any unpleasant emotion, such as guilt,
shame, or anger. They're all connected to fear and designed
to shape our behaviour.

If you think about the value of an unpleasant emotion with
an open and critical mind, you'll see clearly how each has at
some level helped humans develop the social structure we
have now. Some of us may not value unpleasant emotions.
Through human development they serve an important role
as they influence human behaviour. Negative emotions such
as shame, guilt, and anger all have desirable outcomes when
we look at them objectively. Every unpleasant emotion stops
or starts some behaviour. What value does the guilt emotion have? When a person knowingly does something wrong
and afterward experiences guilt, this emotion can become a
deterrent to repeating the behaviour. Guilt, in this case, contributes to preventing a negative behaviour and helps build
social structures.

Moving past any unpleasant emotion begins with understanding that it's nothing more than information. It doesn't
define what we think or do. Like any emotion, regret is a
neurochemical reaction that captures our attention through
feelings. But many struggle to deal with unpleasant emotions
because we've been conditioned, through observing others,
to believe that they're bad and best avoided. As a result, many
people don't have skills or strategies to effectively navigate
unpleasant emotions like regret, which can negatively affect
emotional well-being when not managed.

My first degree was in physical education. Since then, I've been interested in how people overestimate their capacity to engage in physical activity, and I observed this play out in my time as a university football coach. Over my ten years of coaching, each year about a dozen players would come to football camp tryouts unprepared because they had done little or nothing over the summer to improve their physical fitness. Those players would do poorly on their testing, and this was often followed by emotional upset about their performance. They behaved as if they couldn't believe how poorly they had done. In such cases, I would often say something like, "It seems you're frustrated about your performance. What's most frustrating for you?" After some back and forth, the common theme would come out that if they had done more work over the summer, their performance could have been better. These players all experienced regret and other unpleasant emotions like anger, shame, guilt, anxiety, and sadness. Most came to the same conclusion: "I should have trained harder." As painful as this moment was for these young athletes, it was an opportunity to learn and grow from their regret. With regret, it's not the unpleasant emotion that's the major issue; it's what we do when we experience it that matters most for our emotional well-being.

I've seen firsthand how some players used this experience as a lightning rod to motivate their training for the next session. Others didn't get the lesson and came back the following year with the same result, experiencing the same unpleasant emotions. After thirty years, many more of the players who trained and prepared for football camp have become successful professionals than those who showed up unprepared to be their best. I know, as I keep track of many of these men who have become CEOs, doctors, business owners, lawyers, accountants, and professional football players.

REFLECTION

- Do you have a training-camp example where you over-estimated your ability and failed?

- What did you do with this regret?

Regret can be defined as a negative emotion that can impede you from moving forward.[1] It's an intense, unpleasant emotion rooted in self-blame around a decision and action,[2] and it's driven by the belief that you could have prevented it if you had done something differently.[3] The intensity of regret or any other unpleasant emotion depends on the situation's perceived value and importance to us and the people involved. The degree of loss determines the level of emotional pain and the time and energy required to heal. It's common when experiencing regret to replay it with some form of negative self-talk: "I should have done ____ differently." Replaying magnifies the feelings of regret that may be accompanied by other unpleasant emotions such as rejection, shame, and grief.

Regret often has nothing to do with facts, which is why it's referred to as a counterfactual emotion.[4] Counterfactual emotions occur after a person experiences a situation and then determines that things could have turned out better—based on their perceptions, not facts—if they had made a different decision.[5] The unpleasant emotion of regret becomes the comparison between an actual outcome and a better outcome that could have occurred if a different choice had been made.[6]

Heuristics, the mental shortcuts the brain creates to solve problems and make judgements quickly, can result in knee-jerk decisions when we're faced with an unpleasant emotion.[7]

These decisions can compound a situation, creating more unpleasant emotions. This happens because the heuristic is based on flawed information (e.g., "People should always..."). After the event, heuristics can then create an automatic thought (e.g., "I should have..."). This is hindsight bias, when we look back at an event we did not predict and determine it was easily predictable.[8] Hindsight bias can fuel negative, critical self-judgement and blame.

A typical example is that when a person feels regret, they may also experience disappointment. Like regret, this emotion is counterfactual, resulting in a line of thinking in which we wish the events of a situation we're experiencing could have turned out differently.[9] With disappointment, it's common to perceive a situation as outside our locus of control (i.e., the degree to which we believe we have control).[10] The disappointment may be coming from a sense that the situation and circumstances could have been handled differently if only *others* would have done something differently. Regret, on the other hand, is perceived as something inside our locus of control, so *we* could have done something differently.

Regret falls under the sadness dimension of unpleasant (or negative) emotions, according to research by Anna Rowe and Julie Fitness (Figure 2).[11] This is important for you to be aware of because, since regret is linked to sadness, it means it is an emotion that isolates. It is common for a person with sadness to withdraw from others. One reason is for self-protection from any more risk of rejection, failure, and so on. Also, when we experience regret, it is possible onlookers may not know or understand what we are feeling, unlike with anger or fear, where the emotions can often be seen in the person's physiognomy—their expression.

When I'm asked how to help a parent or family member filled with regret on their deathbed, my response is there's no magic solution other than loving them and being there for

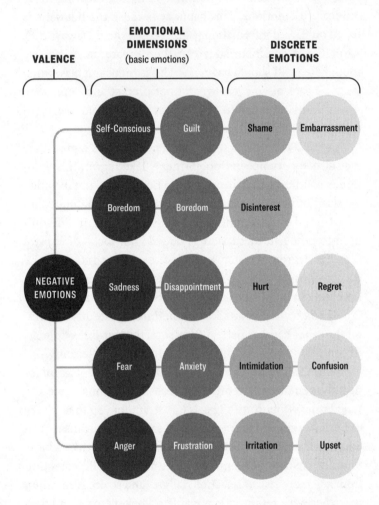

FIGURE 2. NEGATIVE EMOTION DIMENSIONS.

Adapted from Anna Rowe and Julie Fitness, "Understanding the Role of Negative Emotions in Adult Learning and Achievement: A Social Functional Perspective," *Behavioral Science* (2018).

them with a kind ear. In that moment, it's too late. They've missed their opportunity to deal with their regrets.

New research has found that humans' most enduring regret is not living up to the person they wanted to be because they lived their lives based on their duties and responsibilities.[12]

Three things influence our beliefs of what we want out of life:[13]

- Our actual selves: who we think we are

- Our "ought" selves: who we think we should be (e.g., based on current responsibilities and obligations)

- Our ideal selves: our goals, hopes, and dreams for this life

What we do regarding each of these plays a role in our emotional well-being. Taking an inventory of how we respond to each influence can provide insight into why we may be prone to experiencing regret.

Today Matters

Our daily microdecisions and actions shape our emotional well-being. One incredible insight is becoming aware of and realizing the *power of now*. Our lives are happening right now! What we believe to be true today will influence what we do in the future. Our past is our reality: it has happened, and there is no amount of emotional churn or pain we can endure that will change a past failure. When we learn to deal with emotional wounds from regret and other unpleasant emotions, we can free ourselves to become emotionally well. There may be no better medicine than feeling emotionally well. Our mental state is calmer, helping us perceive life situations and challenges positively rather than be paralyzed by fear-based emotions.

Preparing for a life with no regrets requires opening our minds to the possibility that we can do things now or differently to feel better. Though we didn't have to be taught how to feel regret, it's helpful to become more mindful and aware of its nuances to better notice it and have context for constructively challenging regrets.

As I mentioned in the introduction, most regrets fall into one of two buckets:

- Things we regret because we didn't try to do them

- Things we tried that didn't work out as we planned, and we blame ourselves partially or fully

Both kinds of regret can impair our emotional well-being. One study found that 75 percent of respondents regretted not trying something they had wanted to try.[14] Living life to the fullest may not be realistic, but why not make it a goal? Through self-awareness and taking accountability for our life decisions, we can lower the risk of becoming trapped in regret.

A foundational tenet for emotional well-being is discovering and accepting that we own our decisions and behaviours. Though we can't control all the situations that happen in our lives, we are always accountable for our responses. We always have a choice. What's hard to accept is that not all choices will be positive, easy to make, or desirable. Learning how to make better choices requires the right mindset, knowledge, and skills. Many people get trapped in bad decisions by faulty belief systems, negative thoughts, and unpleasant emotions because they don't have emotional well-being skills.

Our mental state influences how we perceive the world and how others observe our general mood (e.g., "Janice seems to be in a good mood today."). The following are five factors that I've found from my clinical experience can predict mental state and influence general mood:

- **Physiology**—Energy level, fatigue, and substances (e.g., drugs and alcohol) directly influence our mental state. Becoming emotionally overwhelmed by stress and filled with cortisol can increase anxiety and tense feelings, which can negatively influence our mental state. The degree of attention we put toward nutrition, movement, and hydration can have a positive effect on our mental state.

- **Focus**—What we focus on influences our mental state. The percentage of time we spend focusing on things we don't like affects the amount of unpleasant emotions and thoughts we experience that can lead to a negative mindset. Similarly, focusing on opportunities, goals, and desires contributes to a positive mental state.

- **Internal dialogue**—What we say to ourselves about our worth, ability, or potential is what we will believe. The more our words about ourselves are positive ("I can" versus "I can't"), the more likely we can create a positive mental state.

- **Circumstances**—The environment we live and work in, our life challenges, the character of the people around us, and our supports influence our mental state. Being around positive and motivated people can have a profound effect on our general mindset and mood. I often tell clients looking to find more peace and happiness to pick their friends wisely and avoid people who are constantly negative and in conflict until they change for the good.

- **Emotional well-being fitness**—Like developing a muscle, improving your emotional well-being through microskills and following a daily mental fitness plan can help you build your resiliency and cope better with unpleasant emotions and unforeseen life circumstances.

Our mood and perception of life situations, in turn, directly influence our decisions and actions.

Do you know anyone who is a night snacker? If so, have you noticed they know this habit's not good for them but believe they can't stop? Over time, this often results in extra weight and increased body fat, leading to unpleasant emotions such as guilt. Guilt arises after someone does something they know is not desirable, and its goal is to stop them from repeating the behaviour. Their mental state plays a role here, however. Believing they can't stop a behaviour prevents them from learning to do anything differently.

When we can change our mental state so that we believe it's possible to gain new knowledge and skills, it better positions us to deal with unpleasant emotions constructively. When we experience guilt while in the right mental state, we can accept what we did wrong, fix our mistake (e.g., practise self-compassion using affirmations such as "It's okay; slips happen."), and commit to not repeating the behaviour. Dealing with regret is more complex, since it requires the mental state of accountability. It also requires us to either learn what is the most appropriate behaviour for us to reduce the risk of experiencing regret or find the courage to overcome a fear that has prevented us from trying.

REFLECTION

- What comes to mind when you think about regret?
- What is your single biggest regret?
- How is this regret affecting you?

Regret is a personal emotion, meaning two people in the same situation, such as a romantic relationship, can have different experiences. For example, after a couple who has been together for two years ends their relationship, one may spend months in regret, thinking about something they did and could have done differently. The other may have no regrets and use the experience to make their next relationship better.

Ignoring regret will have a negative impact on emotional well-being over time. Ample evidence suggests that regret left unchecked can destroy a person's life.[15] This can explain why some people become dependent on drugs, develop other kinds of addictive behaviours, or even engage in suicide attempts.[16] Regret itself isn't bad; it signals an opportunity. In fact, no unpleasant emotion is bad. These emotions guide us in making decisions for our survival. Trying to avoid unpleasant emotions will often have a negative impact on the emotional well-being that defines our mental health. Learning to live with no regrets begins with understanding regret and dealing with it positively.

2

Regret Check-In

M ALCOLM GLADWELL suggests in his book *Blink: The Power of Thinking without Thinking* that after about ten years of tacit skill development, most of us develop a unique skill in our subject area of experience: we can anticipate an outcome with little information.[1] Gladwell refers to this as "thin slicing." One thin-slicing example I regularly experience with new clients is how quickly I can detect regret. Without someone telling me their full story, my gut senses the person is experiencing some regret that has yet to be resolved or defined, and that regret may explain why they're experiencing mental health challenges.

I ask a discovery question, something like, "What rocks may be in your shoes as you've been walking through life over the last number of days, weeks, months, and years?" In response, I rarely get, "What rocks and shoes are you talking about?" The typical response highlights some level of regret about something they did or didn't do regarding a habit, job, career, or relationship. This one question has often helped me work with the client to shine a light on regret, which creates an opportunity for action. Naming the regret allows me to explore how it's affecting the person's emotions, thoughts, and current circumstances.

Imagine walking every day with a sharp rock in your shoe. Besides wearing a hole in your sock, what would that rock do to your foot over time? It could cause real damage, to the point where taking a step forward might feel impossible because the pain would be intolerable.

Case Study: The Unfinished Degree

Manon feels trapped in her job. She doesn't feel valued or recognized by her employer. Her biggest career regret is that she didn't finish her university degree, which would have provided her with more career mobility. Each day when she comes home from work, she takes care of her children, and when things are quiet at night, she often wonders how her life could be different.

Manon is struggling to find a sense of emotional well-being. She now feels trapped in her role because of financial pressure and parenting responsibilities. Numb to her emotional pain, she engages in the maladaptive behaviour (at-risk coping) of night snacking on potato chips to feel better. She knows that eating a large bag of chips each night alone in front of the TV is not good for her. She tells herself she needs to stop but never seems to have the emotional capacity to do so. The consequence is she keeps buying chips as if they were her feel-good medicine. As she puts on extra pounds, she experiences more and more shame, guilt, and regret for not taking charge of this night-snacking habit, all because she failed to focus on her limited career choices due to gaps in her education.

Can you relate to Manon on any level? Notice how regrets can stack on top of one another. Whether Manon knows it, she's coping with a "big R regret"—career choice—that has played a role in creating a new, daily "little R regret"—night snacking.

If you were to provide Manon with advice, what would it be? What regret would you coach Manon on starting to deal with first, and why?

If Manon were in my office today and facing a big and little regret, we would decide where we could start to reduce her emotional discomfort. We likely would agree that it makes the most sense for her to start with the little R first. Why? So she could gain some confidence to take charge of her life through microdecisions and actions. She has direct control of the little R regret. In addition, improving her physical health could give her more energy and confidence to figure out how to improve her education and career.

Little R regrets that we engage in every day have many forms, such as "Why do I keep eating potato chips?" "Why did I overreact again and send that email?" and "Why did I have to say that to her?" These can accumulate and, if not addressed, negatively affect relationships and health.

REFLECTION

- What is one example of a little R regret you do over and over?
- Do you think you can resolve it on your own?

Exploring Big R Regrets

Roese and Summerville introduced what they called twelve life domains.[2] Most big R regrets fall into one of them:

- Career: employment (e.g., "If only I were an accountant.")

- Community: volunteer work (e.g., "I should have volunteered more.")

- Education: level (e.g., "If only I had gone to university.")

- Parenting: style (e.g., "If only I'd spent more time with my children.")

- Family: relationships (e.g., "I wish I'd called my brothers more.")

- Finance: savings (e.g., "I wish had invested in my retirement earlier.")

- Friends: social connections (e.g., "I wish I had focused more on my relationships.")

- Health: diet and exercise (e.g., "If only I had focused on my physical health earlier.")

- Leisure: passions (e.g., "I wish I had travelled when I had my health.")

- Romance: emotional bond (e.g., "I wish I could have maintained an intimate bond with my partner.")

- Spirituality: meaning of life (e.g., "I wish I'd found spirituality earlier.")

- Self: personal development (e.g., "I wish I had focused more on my emotional intelligence.")

Any of these can create the kinds of regret that can become big rocks in your shoe when not dealt with. These rocks will not go away unless you decide to make some life corrections and challenge yourself to deal with your unpleasant emotions—including regret—head-on.

Any type of regret left unchecked can strain your emotional well-being. One study asked an interesting question about regret: "Do you have something you didn't do in your life that you regret?" Of the sample population asked, 74 percent confirmed they had something they regretted not doing.[3] In combination with my clinical experience, this kind of research suggests there are likely many people who do not have a plan to navigate unpleasant emotions.

Regret Inventory

You likely have things in your life you've done that aren't resolved (past regrets) and you haven't tried (unfilled regrets)—big R regrets. You may also have some little R regrets that are behavioural and are fixable mistakes (e.g., acting out based on emotions) or unwanted habits (e.g., night snacking). To discover them, review the regret inventory below.

As you complete the inventory, regardless of the type of regret, avoid over-thinking. Just write down what jumps into your head. The goal is to become aware of your life regrets. Be mindful of both things you haven't done yet and things you haven't resolved. The Zeigarnik effect contends the brain will store regrets of inaction with more intensity than regrets for things we've done.[4]

For each of the twelve life domains, describe a big R regret in one sentence. Be clear whether this is a past or unfulfilled regret. Then, respond to the statement, "I wish I had made a better choice," with a rating on a scale of 1 (very untrue) to 5 (very true). This will tell you which regrets are affecting you most.

Career

_____

_____

Rating: ____

Community

_____

_____

Rating: ____

Education

_____

_____

Rating: ____

Parenting

_____

_____

Rating: ____

Family

_____

_____

Rating: ____

Finance

_____

_____

Rating: ____

Friends

_____

_____

Rating: ____

Health

_____

_____

Rating: ____

Leisure

_____

_____

Rating: ____

Romance

_____

_____

Rating: ____

Spirituality

_____

_____

Rating: ____

Self

_____

_____

Rating: ____

Next, list a maximum of three little R regrets. What is a typical behaviour that often results in feelings of regret (e.g., sending an email; comments you make to a partner)? Rate how each regret negatively affects your quality of life on a scale of 1 (low) to 5 (high).

1 _____

_____

Rating: _____

2 _____

_____

Rating: _____

3 _____

_____

Rating: _____

Finally, list an at-risk behaviour or habit (e.g., drinking; night snacking) that you continue to do even though you're concerned about it. Rate how this regret negatively affects your quality of life on a scale of 1 (low) to 5 (high).

_____

_____

Rating: _____

Where to Start

There's no need to do any formal analysis of your results. You need only notice your regrets without judgement. The closer to 5 on the scale, the higher the level of regret. Notice what emotions you're feeling when you complete this activity and how they're connected to your thoughts. Also notice what at-risk behaviours you may use to help cope with your regrets.

Before beginning your emotional well-being journey, it's prudent to read all of the "ingredient" sections presented in this book. Why? Because each will provide you with new insights that can help you gain perspective and learn some actions so you can take charge of your emotional well-being. After you've reviewed all five ingredients, the next call to action will be to begin your journey to emotional well-being by confronting any regrets or unpleasant emotions that are disrupting your well-being. I suggest you start with a bottom-up approach by first dealing with any unwanted behavioural issues, followed by little R regrets, to prepare to confront your big R regrets.

3

The Regret Snare

EGRET IS not always a linear process with a clear beginning, middle, and end. Some people can get caught in regret for weeks, days, and years. Deciding to move out of regret is not necessarily easy, though in some cases we can quickly decide to do so by saying to ourselves, "I'm not going to take any more time before I move on." When unpleasant emotions like regret take hold and there's no frame of reference for moving forward, we can become stuck, a situation I call the regret snare.

What Is the Regret Snare?

The regret snare is a mental state that can happen when experiencing regret that, if not managed, can have a negative impact on emotional well-being and quality of life. A person who regrets not trying to achieve something in life may end up engaging in at-risk behaviours to cope with their regret. Avoiding life challenges or things we want that create unpleasant emotions often will result in more unpleasant emotions.

Many clients stuck in regret engage in consistent behaviours, but no two may experience regret the same way. I find the regret snare a useful way to understand how a person can live with regret much longer than they want and create unhealthy habits and belief systems about their potential and future. I also use it to help teach clients how regret can become an unconscious habit that does not serve their emotional well-being.

The regret snare involves three independent loops of *replay*, *fantasy*, and *negative coping behaviours* (Figure 3). These activities all revolve within the regret experience loop until the person is able to *accept and release* the regret. Coping skills and emotional well-being determine which of the three loops someone experiences and how long they are caught in the regret snare. The better one's emotional well-being, the faster they'll be able to problem solve and get to the point where they can accept and release a regret, such as the loss of a relationship. Once they get to that point, they can learn to challenge themselves to move past the regret.

Experience—The brain is constantly comparing what we *want* to what we *have*. We have a set of internal pictures of what we would and would not like to have happen. Dr. William Glasser, the author of *Choice Theory*, taught that many of us have a hard time articulating what we want, but we're often clear on what we don't want.[1]

Whenever we experience what we don't want and determine why we did or did not do something, it triggers regret. How long we experience regret depends on our emotional well-being. A high level of emotional well-being is favourable for having the confidence to move past regret.

With regret comes a negative internal dialogue (the harsh things we say to ourselves). When the inner critic goes into

FIGURE 3. THE REGRET SNARE.

self-attack mode, it leads to other unpleasant emotions like shame, anger, guilt, and sullenness.

Dealing with any unpleasant emotion requires accepting that it's neither good nor bad—just an emotion sending information for us to act on. What we do with the information shapes our emotional well-being and mental health. In *The Wisdom of Insecurity: A Message for an Age of Anxiety,* Alan Watts offers a profound thought for navigating difficult emotional moments.[2] Instead of figuring out how to create certainty and security, just accept that there's nothing in life we can count on other than the moment we're in. Tolerating unpleasant emotions involves learning to live with them, and when we know how to stop fighting them, they have much less of a hold on us. "Tolerating unpleasant emotions" may sound like a paradox because, for many, our instinct is to do whatever is necessary to avoid, numb, or hide from them.

Moving past any unpleasant emotion, particularly regret, begins with self-awareness, followed by accountability and action. Most of us have had a minor regret that didn't overwhelm us. In these situations, we didn't feel a need to react. We observed it, didn't fight it but instead accepted it, and then released it by saying something like, "Oh well, next time I will…" At that moment, we learned from the experience and moved on. It's important to note that not all regrets will stay in the regret loop; many will come in and leave quickly, as in this scenario.

Releasing regret does not happen automatically, nor is it a linear process. How we manage regret comes down to our emotional well-being. We're human, and we make mistakes, so we have regrets. There's nothing wrong with that. However, regret can become a problem the longer we're caught in the regret snare. Ignoring or avoiding a regret doesn't change it or its impact on our emotional well-being. An unresolved regret can, and often will, result in more unpleasant emotions and thoughts than are necessary.

Replay—When regret feels overwhelming, we sometimes go into replay mode, where we replay a situation over and over in hopes of better understanding what happened and why. Replaying a situation can help with self-awareness and determining what can be improved. However, it can consume a lot of energy and time and be a cognitive distraction at home and work, resulting in missing healthy experiences and opportunities. The replay loop can be a drain on emotional well-being when we're stuck in it for a long time. It prolongs unpleasant emotions that increase the amount of negative self-talk. Such self-talk may shape a negative belief system about our self-worth because it causes us to re-experience a regret. The ingredients in Part B will provide insights into how to better manage your emotions and thoughts to help you get out of replay mode when you decide you have what you need.

Fantasy—Sometimes, when we're experiencing a regret, we can move into the fantasy loop and spend time and energy thinking about all the what-ifs and how a situation could have turned out differently ("If only they did ____, then ____."). Fantasy can help create thinking about what you may want to focus on or what skill you could benefit from developing. However, it does nothing to change the past or your current reality. Moving out of fantasy requires accepting that we can't change what happened; we can only seek to understand it and learn what better choices we can make in the future. I've seen some clients spend years in this mindset, believing that thinking about the past will somehow change it and lead to a better outcome for them today. The Realization ingredient discussed in Part B can help you determine how to think about and process regret so you can live each day with intention.

Negative coping behaviours—We tend to perceive unpleasant emotions as something bad, like a splinter. Not knowing how to navigate these emotions is why many of us engage in maladaptive (at-risk) coping behaviours to either escape or numb emotional pain. Engaging in at-risk behaviours can result in secondary problems such as addiction. Whether the behaviour involves food, gambling, social media, substances, shopping, or work, it serves the same purpose: to cope with emotional pain.

Accept and release—How much effort it takes to break out of the regret snare depends on your emotional well-being. Neuroscience has found that regret activates the anterior insula and dorsomedial prefrontal cortex of the brain in decision making.[3] Intense dislike of a perceived loss or missed opportunity can trigger motivation. When we're open and ready, we can learn and grow from unwanted life experiences so something doesn't happen again or we at least try to do the best we can, since avoiding something we want can become a major life regret.

REFLECTION

Pick one thing you experienced regret about in the past that you no longer feel. Run this experience through the following regret snare framework:

1 What mental loops within the regret snare did you experience?
2 How much time did you spend in each mental loop?
3 How did you get out of each mental loop?
4 Was it hard for you to break out of the regret snare?
5 How has this regret helped you?

One of my favourite summer jobs as a university student was coastal search and rescue with the Canadian Coast Guard. It was a fantastic opportunity to learn to navigate in the thick fog that often blankets the Atlantic coast. Without the right equipment, it's impossible to get a sense of direction at sea in a dense fog. Not having a chart plotter and compass can make it challenging to find safe shores.

The regret snare can put a person in a dense fog of unpleasant emotion that impedes them from finding sunshine and blue skies. What removes emotional fog is self-awareness: the first step toward taking charge of unpleasant emotions like regret. Self-awareness is not a cure, but it is an important factor. Moving out of the regret snare begins with knowing you're in it.

4

A Gift or a Curse: You Decide

L IVING WITH no regrets requires managing unpleasant emotions. It's important to keep in mind that any unpleasant emotion can result in regret. For example, you might get angry at a sibling and not deal with your anger, or you might feel guilty for not apologizing for something you did wrong. Think about the consequences of not dealing with an unpleasant emotion and the risk of regret. We have, on average, 25,000 days to live the way we want. Regardless of the situation, we always have free will. Our past does not define us; what we choose to do each day determines our emotional well-being. Thinking about life is helpful, but we only live the life we want by making decisions to get on our desired path.

Fear is what drives all unpleasant emotions. In *Think Like a Monk*, Jay Shetty shares wisdom from his experiences studying to be a monk. One of his critical insights into finding inner peace was to not avoid fear.[1] Avoiding fear allows it to fester and grow. Managing unpleasant emotions begins with neither reacting to nor running from them. Accepting this wisdom, discovering how not to fight unpleasant emotions, and learning how to notice them can put us on the path to growing our emotional well-being.

Regardless of how prepared we think we are regarding our health, relationships, career, and family, things can go contrary to our plans, and negative stress results. Only we can decide how we'll respond. As you saw with the regret snare, unpleasant emotions don't always leave as fast as they come. We'll remain in a loop of distress until we find a resolution or a way to soothe the emotion in a manner that does not harm us or put our mental health at risk. When we experience emotions like guilt, shame, anger, and regret, remember this is nothing more than a chemical reaction telling us that it's in our best interest to move away from a perceived fear. By developing a positive mindset, we can learn that unpleasant emotions are not evil; their purpose is to protect us. They don't need to create mental harm.

Most of us don't want to fail in our job, since this can be a risk factor for steady employment and can disrupt our financial health. Getting feedback that we're failing can trigger a negative stress response. Our emotional well-being and our confidence in our ability to find new employment affect how we experience fear when we learn that our job is at risk.

Case Study: The Lost Job

Frank lost his job because of his poor attendance. He had a history of being late for work. His manager had talked with him about it many times and had provided verbal warnings and a written warning. He liked Frank but felt he was showing no signs of improvement, especially considering all the feedback Frank had received that he must change his behaviour.

Frank's manager and human resources got fed up and decided to fire him.

Frank realized he had lost his job due to poor decision making and not accepting and acting on the feedback. His regret was mixed in with several other unpleasant emotions: sorrow, hurt, grief, anger, self-blame, frustration, and disappointment.[2] They amplified and contributed to his pessimistic mood.

Frank's outlook about his future employment is bleak. He's caught in the regret snare and is constantly replaying his mistake. His opportunity for self-correction is to learn from this mistake so he doesn't repeat it in his next job. Not knowing how to leverage regret to evolve, however, Frank is being held back from finding a new job by the regret snare. To move forward, he must acknowledge his mistake and accept that he can't change the past. He needs to be open to learning so he can do better in the future, to ensure this kind of employment mistake doesn't happen again.

We can't expect to live our lives successfully without dealing with regret along the way. Failure is a part of life, and no amount of hope will reduce this fact. Wanting something and trying hard to get it doesn't mean we're not going to blow it. We must accept that regret is a normal part of the human experience to be able to benefit and grow from it. No matter how many times we think about something, we can never change history; we can only learn from it. Living with no regrets means accepting that we'll make mistakes at the most inconvenient times. How we cope will determine how we experience the loss.

My motivation for writing this book was the fact that unpleasant emotions, especially regret, can be strong teachers when we're open to learning. Researcher Neal Roese of the Kellogg School of Management at Northwestern University found that young people rated regret more favourably than unfavourably because it motivated corrective action.[3] Roese's research suggests that regret, out of all the unpleasant emotions, motivates people to make sense of the world, abstain from future negative behaviour, gain insight, achieve social harmony, and improve their ability to act on desired opportunities. Regret, then, can be a gift. Being open to regret is a motivator for acquiring knowledge and skills for corrective action, such as modifying an ineffective habit or behaviour or making a different decision in a similar situation to achieve a more desirable outcome.[4]

There are different intensities of regret. Stubbing your toe hurts, but breaking it hurts more. However, in both situations, your toe is sore. Unpleasant emotions often get our attention quickly, but predicting who will experience prolonged regret is challenging because it depends on the perceptions, expectations, and desires of the person involved. Two people in the same situation can have two completely different experiences.

Case Study: Different Work Approaches

Two employees sell insurance products in the corporate sector. Angela is hyper-focused on her career advancement. She wants a promotion to a senior manager role and believes she has done all the right things to get there. She went to what she considered the right school to get the right degree and completed the correct summer internships. She constantly thinks about moving upward in her career, so she pushes herself hard every day. She's more than willing to work long hours as she wants to demonstrate her commitment to top performance results. Her motivation is to get ahead.

Regine has a much more laid-back approach to her career. She has lots of interests outside of work that are as important to her as her job. She's happy doing what she's doing and isn't super motivated to push herself much harder than she does. However, she cares about doing a good job, tries her best every day, and is well-liked and respected by the team and clients she works with.

Angela and Regine have been selected to make their biggest pitch ever to a large corporate client. They work well together preparing for the presentation and feel that it went well. Both leave the meeting feeling they have a good shot at winning this new account that would certainly get attention at the corporate head office.

Four days later, they find out they didn't get the account. Angela is upset, starts to think about all the things she could have done differently, and is filled with regret. Regine thinks it's too bad; it would have been nice to win. However, she believes she did her best and there will be a next time.

The key takeaway from this case study is that regret is subjective, and our expectations can set us up for regret. Expecting that we must be perfect and things must always work out can strain our emotional well-being. Angela's regret may be self-induced because she hadn't created any space for the possibility that she would not get the outcome she wanted. If she gets locked down in regret, she can end up spending time in the regret snare, replaying a situation to the point where she misses parts of her life.

Our expectations and desires influence our emotional well-being. Having a clearly defined life course can help create expectations to live life based on core values and purpose. This action helps to set our internal expectations that will influence how we react. For Regine, work is important. However, her mindset made her less likely to experience regret than Angela because she recognizes that doing her best is all she can control.

Having explored the concept of regret and how it relates to other unpleasant emotions, you now have context. Context is a critical factor in emotional well-being because it gives you an opportunity to remove self-judgement and opens the door for self-compassion, which creates the condition for learning. The five ingredients provide actions you can take to learn how to better manage unpleasant emotions.

MAKING A PLAN FOR DEALING WITH REGRET

I guess I would rather
regret the things
I've done than regret the
things I've never done.

LUCILLE BALL

THIS PART is designed to assist you in deciding what skills you can develop to move past regret or to move forward and take action so you have no regrets for not trying. The following key topics will be covered in this section:

- How to leverage the brain's full potential
- How to navigate negative emotions
- How to influence your automatic thoughts in your favour
- How to break unhealthy, at-risk coping behaviours
- How to develop an action plan for moving past regret or living with no regrets

Realization

Information
Influences How
We Experience
the World

We need to learn to want what we have, not to have what we want, to get stable and steady happiness.

ATTRIBUTED TO THE DALAI LAMA

YOU'RE IN the back seat of a car that's rolling down a hill. The fear and terror you experience as the car gains speed and the feeling of having no control can be what it's like when we we're flooded with an unpleasant emotion. Without context on how to stop, navigate, or manage the unpleasant emotion, we can feel powerless and like our life is crashing in on us. Sometimes, a regret due to something we did or did not do can create internal churn that fuels other unpleasant emotions. These emotions can train the brain to be more sensitive and negative than necessary, directly affecting emotional well-being.

One way to be able to reach the brake pedal and regain control is to learn some basic information on how the brain works. The brain is a dynamic, living organism that is constantly analyzing and learning. Emotions are like the lights on a dashboard and the alarms that notify us of an issue. They don't make decisions; they create attention. How we react to emotion depends on how well we understand the control we have over our reactions.

The Realization ingredient provides insights and microskills that can sway the brain to do what we want, rather than leave us feeling powerless. The brain is a powerful tool. Not understanding how it works can mean we are unable to leverage its capacity to our advantage. When we learn to calm our mind, we can see the world differently and find hope and the path to our desired outcomes.

The Realization ingredient will cover the following key points:

- How the brain works
- How it supports emotional well-being
- How we can influence our brain instead of react to it

5

Why Knowing about the Brain Matters

'VE NEVER attempted to build a house, and there are good reasons why. Like having no knowledge or skills in carpentry, concrete, plumbing, electrical, planning, and design, as a starter. Even using Google, I have zero chance. I'm not being hard on myself, just honest. But I can create a mental vision of what I would want the house to look like.

A significant percentage of the population is struggling with mental health, and even more with emotional well-being. Why? One reason is aligned with my house analogy. To build a house with our own hands requires the proper knowledge and skills. Likewise, developing positive emotional well-being and reducing the chance of mental illness requires specific competency.

Our brain is one of the most critical tools for learning how to manage emotional well-being. This may sound obvious, but is it? What do you know about how your brain works? If you're like most of us, not a lot. Okay, before you read on, I'm not suggesting you need to have any deep knowledge. I know from my experience helping people that when they get just some basic insights, it helps them normalize their experience and encourages them to learn what they can do to get their brains working for them rather than against them.

If you're like me, when you pick up your TV remote control and press the On button, you expect the TV to turn on. If it doesn't, I start randomly pressing buttons. Though there's a manual that shows how to use the remote control, I often don't know where it is.

When we get overwhelmed and our emotional well-being is not where we want it to be, doing things that are like randomly pushing buttons on a remote control in hopes of feeling better is leaving a lot to chance. When it comes to knowing how our brain works, most of us are not even aware that there's a manual. The Realization ingredient offers some fundamental insights into brain function that can provide perspective and help us make better decisions.

REFLECTION

- If you're concerned about unwanted stress, you can determine your stress baseline by completing the Stress-Load Monitor in Appendix A. Consider doing this monthly for six months to track your progress.

- Unwanted stress impairs cognitive functions, concentration, memory, attention, problem solving, and decision making.[1] How we train our brain to process stress influences how well we cope with it.

Insights into How the Brain Works

The human brain is a tad more complex than a TV remote control. Having some primary knowledge of how the brain works can moderate your reactions to negative emotions and thoughts. This knowledge can help you to act, instead of feeling powerless and accepting whatever your brain offers. You don't need to train as a psychologist, brain surgeon, or neuropsychologist; you just need some tips that can help you make some tweaks. When I get stuck on my computer and it's acting wonky, I've learned to pause, breathe, and reboot. It works about 95 percent of the time—not perfect, but better than randomly hitting keys and getting upset.

The brain has created both pleasant and unpleasant emotions through human evolution to aid in keeping us alive. Emotions' evolutional function is to drive coping and adaptive behaviour.[2] They're found in subcortical areas of the brain (amygdala and the ventromedial prefrontal cortices), which produce biochemical reactions that affect our physical state. For the most part, they operate in our subconscious and come to the surface based on stimuli, situations, and thoughts.

The goal of all pleasant and unpleasant emotions is to motivate a potential adaptive behaviour to help us enjoy or deal with a presenting interpersonal or intrapersonal conflict. Emotions can shape and influence our cognition, physiology, behaviour, and subjective experiences.[3] Emotional responses trigger the motivation for our behavioural choice to approach or withdraw from a situation.

Feelings are less specific than emotions. Feelings happen in the neocortical regions of the brain and influence what happens after we experience a particular emotion. For example, how we respond to regret is subjective, based on our personal experience, interpretation of a situation, and learned coping skills. What we're generally feeling (the combination of emotions) influences our mental state and mood. If we typically live each day with 70 percent pleasant emotions, we tend to be more chipper than if 30 percent are pleasant.

A helpful analogy I teach my clients is comparing emotional well-being to diabetes. A diabetic's health depends on them balancing their sugar and insulin levels. In emotional well-being, the daily balance is the percentage of time spent in pleasant versus unpleasant emotions. Most of us have yet to grasp that unpleasant emotions themselves are not destructive. Lacking awareness of how and why the brain works, many people do all they can to avoid, numb, and hide from unpleasant emotions, which may be one of the biggest challenges we have and why there's so much mental illness in the world.

The brain's belief system is influenced by daily thoughts that can affect serotonin levels, a hormone that regulates mood, happiness, and anxiety.[4] Serotonin also plays a role in sleep, eating, and digestion. Research suggests that low serotonin levels in the brain can lead to depression and increase the risk of anxiety, suicidal behaviour, and emotional impulsivity.[5] In some cases, I recommend that a client struggling with their mood get their serotonin levels tested to serve as a baseline. As we create their emotional well-being plan, I recommend exploring (with a medical professional) the possibility of adding a serotonin supplement if they're not making enough serotonin naturally. Our daily nutrition can also affect how well the brain works. It operates much better when fed a balanced and healthy diet. In addition to diet, what we focus on and think about influences the brain's emotions, feelings, and mood.

Belief systems are created through the brain's neuroplasticity. The combination of dominant emotions and thinking themes as it processes and experiences the world train the brain to be more positive or negative. This is a simplistic explanation, but just as we don't need to understand all the tech behind how the remote control can send a signal to the TV to turn it on and off, we don't need to understand how the brain's neuroplasticity fires and wires thoughts and emotions—we just need to know that it does.

What we must understand is that our emotional well-being is influenced by what we decide to put into our belief system. We each have the right to program our brain for what we want it to believe. However, we must know this is what we're doing, or we may default to negativity. Many of us have a natural default that's more negative than positive. We can make a massive change to our emotional well-being when we accept that the brain is not fixed and that we can learn how to wire it to be more positive by tweaking our belief system.

Beliefs influence the kind of automatic thoughts we have when faced with a challenging life event. These thoughts influence our emotions, feelings, and mood. What was in the belief system before the event can predict the kinds of automatic thoughts that will occur.

Review each statement below to determine which kind of emotions—positive or negative—you would attach to each thought:

- I'm a good person.
- I know people like me.
- I'm a happy person.
- I want to be a positive person.
- I'm not sure if people will like me.
- I worry about whether I'm good enough.
- I worry that they're trying to take advantage of me.
- I hope they like me.

The first four will elicit pleasant emotions; the second four, unpleasant emotions. As you read on, you will discover how many thoughts you can have each day. (Hint: A lot.) Imagine you have fewer positive than negative thoughts. Will this train your brain to be more positive or negative? The brain is like a muscle: what it focuses on most is what it does best. The more we practise being positive, the more our brain will become hardwired to be positive.

Case Study: Mood Matters

Jasmine and Janice are best friends and have been for over twenty years. Jasmine is happy and optimistic for the most part. Janice is witty and generally pleasant but often presents as being emotionally flat or down. Neither may know why they're different and why Jasmine presents as a happier person than Janice most days. It's to do with how each constructed their belief system.

Compare Jasmine and Janice:

	% of positive thoughts and self-affirmation	% of negative observations about self and others
Jasmine	90%	10%
Janice	50%	50%

Jasmine is better prepared than Janice to cope with unpleasant emotions in a way that doesn't create mental strain. For the next twenty years of their relationship, Janice will keep showing up the way she is if she doesn't change her belief system. By becoming aware of how her belief system shapes her self-confidence and trust, she can learn to better deal with unpleasant emotions.

The Realization ingredient, as well as the ingredients in the coming sections, can help you learn to train your brain to better cope with unpleasant emotions and create more positive thoughts. Not developing emotional well-being skills to cope with unpleasant emotions like regret can, over time, negatively impact your mental health.[6]

REFLECTION

Who are you more like, Jasmine or Janice?

- Over the past thirty days, on a scale of 1 (blue and down) to 3 (okay and getting by) to 5 (chipper and happy), how would you describe your mood on a typical day?

- One way to objectively track your mood is to monitor it over the next ninety days. There's growing evidence that personal informatics (self-tracking personal data) can play a role in supporting focus and attention on improving outcomes.[7]

6

Five Facts You May Not Know about Your Brain

THE MORE you're aware of how your brain works, the more likely you'll be able to make informed rather than emotional decisions. You can train your brain only if you know what to train. As you review each question in this chapter, consider how the insight can help you make better decisions and train your brain to improve your emotional well-being.

On Average, How Many Thoughts Do You Have Each Day?

In meditation, "mindfulness" is often referenced. There's little wonder our minds feel full each day. While research from Queen's University found that the average person has 6,200 thoughts per day,[1] the National Science Foundation reported the number to range from 12,000 to 60,000, 80 percent of which are negative and 95 percent repetitive.[2] Regardless of which data is more accurate, it's evident that the brain does a lot of thinking every day.

Imagine on a typical day that you have thirty negative thoughts about yourself or others. Over time, this can negatively shape your belief system, which is filed in your subconscious brain, outside your awareness, like the dark corners of a basement. How you train your brain influences the kinds of thoughts that will surface from your subconscious brain when under pressure.

Also, consider that regardless of how much you train your brain, negative thoughts may pop up. You need to learn to train it to not accept or believe that every automatic, negative thought is true or correct. Jon Kabat-Zinn teaches that when any negative thought jumps into our head, we should realize that it's most often not true, is laughable, and has zero relevance in defining our life—that it has no more influence on us than what we had for breakfast three days ago.[3] His point is that we need to condition our brain to disbelieve things we know are not good for us (e.g., "I'm not worthy."). Believing these negative thoughts doesn't serve any useful purpose.

To train your brain, pay attention to the number of automatic, negative thoughts you have each day. Practise rejecting critical thoughts by asking questions that enable you to see your current life situation in a more favourable light. The key takeaway is that your brain will learn to do what you tell it, so create more intentional thinking about who you want to be, versus automatically accepting as true whatever random thoughts come up about who you are.

How Much Does Your Mind Wander?

We're constantly inundated by stimuli and information that competes for our attention. Harvard psychologists Matthew Killingsworth and Daniel Gilbert conducted a study with

2,250 subjects, discovering that their minds were wandering 47 percent of the time.[4] This research concluded that a wandering mind is an unhappy mind, and that wandering was the cause, not the consequence, of unhappiness.

"Monkey brain" is a term used in meditation to describe how the brain wanders from topic to topic. One reason it wanders as much as it does is due to the default mode network (DMN), a group of brain regions (medial prefrontal cortex, posterior cingulate cortex, and inferior parietal lobule) that have been critical for our survival. Though this part of our brain plays a role, it's not that helpful for creating happiness and has been linked to anxiety and depression.[5] Designed to protect us, the DMN has the brain constantly wandering to examine thoughts from the past and future. We can better manage the DMN by training the brain through mindful practice that helps us spend more time in the present.

One way to train the brain to be focused on the present is through intentional engagement in activities you enjoy doing. University of Chicago psychologist Mihaly Csikszentmihalyi created the term "flow," which he describes as a peak-performance mental state where every action and decision flows with little effort.[6] This state improves muscle reaction times, pattern recognition, and lateral thinking. The benefits of this practice can tame an overactive DMN.

Engaging in high-value activities is key to creating flow. Minimalism coach Leo Babauta shares nine practical tips for training the brain to find flow:[7]

- **Choose activities you love.** Engage in activities that you value and enjoy and that catch your attention and interest.

- **Choose an important task.** Pick an activity that you find meaningful and a good use of your time so it's more likely your mind will flow doing it.

- **Make sure it's challenging but not too hard.** The activity must be difficult enough to require concentration but never to a level where you feel mentally overwhelmed.

- **Find your quiet, peak time.** Choose a quiet time when you feel you have your peak energy (e.g., early morning).

- **Clear away distractions.** Create success by clearing away distractions to establish quiet time and space for focus (e.g., turn off notifications).

- **Learn to focus on the task for as long as possible.** With patience, planning, and persistence, you'll learn how to stay focused on the task for more extended periods.

- **Enjoy yourself.** Allow yourself to enjoy what you're doing to help you get lost in the activity. You'll know you're in flow when the time seems to fly.

- **Keep practising.** The more you train your brain on this task, the more opportunities you'll have to discover flow and experience its benefits.

- **Reap the rewards.** Enjoy the benefits of getting what you want done while creating more pleasant emotions that support emotional well-being.

Taking charge of what you focus on can play a significant role in training your brain to calm down and concentrate on what you enjoy, which will promote positive emotional well-being.

What Percentage of Daily Activities Are Preprogrammed?

Before you woke up and started your day, approximately 40 percent of your daily activities had been preprogrammed through habits and associative learning.[8] Neuroscientists have found that the habit-making part of the brain, called the basal ganglia, is where all our habits are stored. It plays a role in the development of emotions, memories, and pattern recognition.[9] The basal ganglia allows humans to perform complex behaviours such as driving a car without using much mental energy.

The consequence of so much preprogramming is that we can spend much of our day on autopilot. One study found that 96 percent of samples reported they were living life on autopilot.[10] The researchers suggested that being in a mindless state increases the risk of subconscious decision making that may not always be in our best interest (e.g., poor lifestyle choices and habits). This research also concluded that the average person in the study made fifteen decisions on autopilot each day—more than 250,000 autopilot decisions in a lifetime. Any preprogrammed routine may not be good for you, so ensure your brain doesn't function on autopilot.

Gustavo Razzetti, a corporate culture consultant, provides five signs a person may be living on autopilot:[11]

- They have a predictable routine packed with activities they can easily do without thinking.

- They prioritize pleasing other people, allowing others to make decisions that concern them rather than considering their own happiness.

- They're always "on," so they rarely take time to reflect on their feelings or enjoy pleasurable moments.

- Their typical day is a blur, and they find it difficult to remember what they accomplished.

- They want to have more fun but can't stop their mind from wandering, so they feel they're missing out.

Training the brain to get out of autopilot begins with becoming aware of the possibility that your routines are not good for long-term emotional well-being. Try monitoring your daily actions to determine what you're doing on autopilot. Fear of missing your life and experiencing regret as a result can motivate you to observe what you're doing each day and reduce your risk of running on autopilot. Your goals can also provide you with intention. It can take time to get the things you want, but you can train your brain to recognize that only you can create your life as you want it to be, one decision and one day at a time. Being awake, aware, and focused better positions you to make microdecisions that promote your emotional well-being and align with your values.

What Percentage of Decisions Are Made by Emotions?

Harvard professor Gerald Zaltman's research suggests that 95 percent of all purchase decisions happen in the subconscious brain and are influenced by emotions.[12] This indicates that our attraction to things often occurs outside our conscious mind. The subconscious mind can process 20 million bits of information per second, while the conscious mind processes just forty bits, which means the subconscious mind can process

500,000 times more information per second than the con-scious mind.[13] Because of this, emotional messaging is decoded faster and influences our preferences and decisions. The brain uses emotions to understand what's going on regarding memories, thoughts, and beliefs.[14]

Emotions trigger how we feel, which drives our behaviour. Emotions also influence the decisions we make and the speed with which we make them. They don't tell us what to do. That depends on what the brain tells us, which comes from free will. Unpleasant emotions like regret can pop into our head and be helpful, since they can help the brain to run a rapid simulation of what-ifs. The result of such an exercise may be that we don't act on our emotions to avoid taking risks.[15] Understanding the brain's creation of emotions and thoughts, then, involves two regions. Experiencing anger, for example, doesn't mean we have to react by slapping someone in the face. Anger only creates the urge to decide on an action that will move us away from or toward a situation. The brain can be trained to not react to unpleasant emotions so that we reduce the risk of making poor emotional decisions.

Take these steps to avoid making emotional decisions:

- **Pause.** Train your conscious brain to resist whenever you feel overwhelmed, challenged, or agitated and have an urge to make fast decisions. To avoid making a mistake, leverage the pause to create mental space for time to think before reacting.

- **Prompt fact-based reactions.** Your gut instincts can detect danger. However, when there's no danger, they can cause unnecessary emotional upset. Create a mindset that requires data and facts before you make a decision.

- **Write down a plan before acting on it.** Research suggests that the act of writing thoughts in a journal format makes things clear and supports better decision making.[16]

- **Seek out consensus.** To reduce emotional decision making, run ideas by a trusted peer to get their reaction. If there's consensus on your decision, proceed; if not, consider an alternative.

What Are Cognitive Errors?

When not monitored, the brain can create many thinking errors that result in incorrect conclusions and mistakes. The root cause of these thinking errors is cognitive errors. They occur when the brain assumes something is true without evidence or facts—just what it believes. For example, we might conclude someone didn't return a call because they don't like us, without any other evidence. There could be thousands of reasons why they haven't called that have nothing to do with us.

Nobel Prize–winner Daniel Kahneman's book *Thinking, Fast and Slow* suggests humans do two types of thinking: System 1 (fast) and System 2 (slow).[17] System 1 thinking oversees automatic responses, such as completing the phrase, "like a hot knife through..." Because of System 1, you didn't have to work; you just automatically said "butter."

System 2 involves deep thinking—the kind needed to deal with a complex statistical question or back up a trailer for the first time. It requires focus and cognitive energy. Making kneejerk decisions that trust System 1 thinking results in mistakes and the risk of regret. Slowing down and not rushing to make decisions reduces the risk of making cognitive errors.

Kahneman's work indicates that many thinking errors occur because of bias and accepting things to be true without asking for or validating the facts.[18] One lesson from Kahneman is that humans are too confident that our first thoughts are correct, which increases decision making solely on "what feels right." This approach often results in poor decisions. His sage advice to reduce cognitive errors is to slow down when unsure, avoid the urge to be overly confident, and don't assume that whatever thought pops into your head is the right one.

Consulting psychologist Catherine Hambley provides advice to avoid making cognitive-biased decisions.[19] Her techniques include the following:

- **Be aware.** Accept that humans are prone to thinking errors. Be open to the fact that our own bias can blind us; therefore, it's helpful to focus on being more reflective than reactive.

- **Think about thinking.** Practise metacognition, or thinking about thinking. Become curious, step back from a problem, and ponder how else you might think about it. Doing this can create more mental flexibility and challenge your thinking pattern to reduce thinking errors.

- **Look for options.** One way to prevent mistakes is to never automatically accept the first option that jumps into your head. Insist that you'll consider what other options there may be before deciding. This can spark alternatives and contrasts that can assist in reducing cognitive errors.

- **Practise humility.** Be open to the possibility that you could be wrong. This creates an opportunity to listen, ask questions, and learn from others before deciding.

REFLECTION

- What are the top three nuggets of information about how your brain works that you've learned from this chapter?

- Consider how each can help you improve your emotional well-being.

- Training your brain to do what you want it to do is much better than allowing it to do whatever it wants.

7

Still More Facts about Your Brain

H OW WE perceive the world influences how we experience it. Many of us have had a day when nine things went right and one thing went wrong. How did we evaluate the day? It's common, when allowed, for the brain to filter out the value of positive experiences and put more attention on negative experiences.[1] The consequence is the brain concludes the day was not a good one because of one negative event.

Can you relate to this example? The more you learn about how your brain works, the more likely you'll learn how to develop your emotional well-being, which positions you to be more objective and make fewer kneejerk, emotional decisions because of a flawed belief system and negative thinking. It's so important to understand that a flawed belief system we create doesn't represent who we are.

When allowed to fire off regularly occurring thinking errors, the brain increases our risk of self-doubt and unnecessary stress. Thinking errors, like cognitive distortions, happen automatically.[2] The brain creates a cognitive distortion by drawing conclusions based on one piece of information while ignoring or not considering other relevant information.

Imagine, for example, you get positive feedback from a client about a presentation you just made in their office. They were over the moon, their enthusiasm and energy perhaps the best response you had received all year from a client. You walk out of their office on cloud nine, feeling proud. On the way back to the office, your colleague suggests you could have done one small thing differently. Without any reflection, you focus on this negative feedback and take it to heart. You then begin to fixate on what you could have done better. The consequence is you automatically become less proud of the client meeting. Without realizing it, you've dismissed the client's feedback and focused more on the negative comment, which is now influencing your mood.

These kinds of cognitive distortions are, in essence, mental filters that shade how we view our world and can negatively influence our mental state and mood.[3] The more we learn not to trust every negative thought that jumps into our head as the most important, the more we can be secure, balanced, and objective in how we evaluate our experiences.[4]

Our ability to make healthy choices relies heavily on the brain's prefrontal cortex, the part that regulates executive function (i.e., higher-order thinking in the absence of emotion) and where self-control and willpower come from. It controls behaviours, not emotions. The frontal lobe operates much like a battery; when it's not charged, it runs less efficiently. Therefore, it's important to practise emotional well-being to keep the brain working at its full potential.

What Is Attachment Theory?

To become an adult, we had to be a child first, and how we behave as an adult is influenced by how we were raised as a child. Attachment theory links our upbringing to how our brain attachment section functions in intimate relationships. The theory provides insights into how people behave in intimate adult relationships. What do you know about the brain's attachment region? Many know little to nothing about it. I suspect this is one factor in why so many relationships end.

Hold Me Tight: Seven Conversations for a Lifetime of Love by Sue Johnson is one of many resources on attachment theory, and it provides a non-academic overview and practical insights into how attachment works within the brain.[5] Suppose you're struggling with trust and feelings of insecurity in an intimate relationship. It could be due to the attachment region of your brain, which stores what intimate relationships mean to you. Attachment theory illuminates how parenting styles install programs into the brain's subconscious mind, often outside our level of awareness.

Parenting programs one of four main attachment styles into adults' brains:

* **Secure attachment style refers** to the ability to form secure, loving relationships with others.[6] The person finds it easy to trust others, be trusted, love and accept love, and get close to others with relative ease.

* **Anxious attachment style is** a form of insecure attachment marked by a deep fear of abandonment.[7] The person tends to be uncertain about their relationships, often worrying that their partner will leave them, and seeks constant validation.

- **Avoidant attachment style is a form of insecure attachment marked by a fear of intimacy.**[8] The person tends to have trouble getting close to or trusting others in relationships.

- **Fearful-avoidant attachment style is a combination of anxious and avoidant attachment styles.**[9] The person is conflicted, as they desperately crave affection but want to avoid it at all costs.

Maintaining a secure and healthy partner relationship has been proven to positively influence mental health and longevity.[10] Attachment theory has helped many couples uncover intimacy issues and learn how to communicate better, close open wounds, use conflict to bond and become closer, and better understand each other and communicate. It helps a person learn how to retrain the attachment region of their brain without shame or judgement and get rid of old, subconscious programming. Attachment theory can help you create a new way to live and communicate within an intimate relationship.[11]

What Are Mirror Neurons?

You're in an excellent mood while walking to a coffee shop to visit a friend. When you meet, they say nothing but stare at you with an angry expression. Your mood starts to shift. You feel the tension, and random thoughts start running in your head: "What's wrong? What did I do?" No one has said a word, and you've already moved from pleasant to unpleasant emotions.

How did this happen? It's because of mirror neurons designed to observe others and then mimic their behaviours.[12]

Mirror neurons run in your brain automatically and can explain why many people unconsciously copy others' behaviours. Mirror neurons facilitate human empathy through a process called brain-to-brain coupling.[13] In the example, you began to match your friend's anger because your mirror neurons plugged you into their emotional state.

When someone smiles at us, we often match them and smile back without noticing. If you smile at someone who doesn't smile back, you may wonder what's up and immediately feel less comfortable. Mark Goulston, the author of *Just Listen: Discover the Secret to Getting Through to Absolutely Anyone*, refers to this as a mirror neuron gap, and it can influence how we interact with others.[14] His point is we don't need to react when someone doesn't return the smile. When we're aware, we're more open to the possibility the person may have something else on their mind that has nothing to do with us.

One way to discover mirror neurons is to notice what others do when you smile at them. Over the next week, smile at five or more people a day and record how many smile back at you. You likely will discover about three out of five do. Those who don't return your smile may be distracted with other thoughts, so don't assume that their lack of acknowledgement has anything to do with you.

Microskills for Thinking about Mirror Neurons

Know the 7–38–55 rule. Remember these three numbers discovered by Albert Mehrabian, a pioneer in non-verbal communication. He found that 7 percent of all communication is words, 38 percent is how we say the words, and 55 percent is non-verbal.[15] Non-verbals matter, so don't underestimate them and the impact they can have on others' moods.

Be aware of social contagion. Humans can spread emotions like a common cold. If you're in the presence of someone negative, be careful not to accept their negative gifts. Emotional contagion can be defined as the spread of mood through exposure to others' moods. Research has shown how social contagion can work automatically. For example, if you get passed while driving, you start to speed up without thinking about it.[16] How does this happen? You automatically begin to mirror the other driver's behaviour by driving faster. Be aware of how you respond to your environment. You have a choice, provided you pay attention to how others' moods influence you.

What Role Does Dopamine Play in Motivating Behaviour?

Dopamine is known as the brain's feel-good neurotransmitter. This pleasure drug plays a vital role in how we feel. It works with other powerful chemicals such as serotonin, endorphins, and oxytocin (i.e., the love chemical), shaping and forming our positive and negative habits. It influences our motivation and cognitive decision making.[17]

Dopamine can trick us into believing at-risk behaviours that are not good for us are okay when we want to feel good. As an example, Mary is having a difficult day and feeling stressed. Her mood is off, and she's in a negative mindset about her work situation. Potato chips are a favourite nighttime snack when watching a movie, so while experiencing more unwanted stress at the end of the day, Mary's brain automatically fires off the urge to get some chips to snack on when she turns on her TV. This unhealthy habit has been installed as a coping strategy to feel good and help her forget the day's events.

To understand this craving, go back in time a bit. Whether Mary knows it, her brain was trained to like potato chips as a feel-good food the first time she tasted them because dopamine is a neurotransmitter that's goal-oriented to find pleasure. Before Mary ate her first potato chip, her brain had no frame of reference for whether it was good or bad. However, once she ate the first one and liked the taste, her brain anchored it by releasing dopamine. Mary didn't have to do anything consciously.

When under distress, Mary's unconscious brain automatically begins to look for solutions to reduce this stress and the unpleasant emotions. What comes up is an urge, followed by a craving for potato chips. This motivation to act increases because with the urge comes a release of dopamine that influences the brain to focus on acquiring potato chips. This behaviour can become an unhealthy habit due to the dopamine reward cycle: When Mary sits in front of the TV, the dopamine fires off in anticipation of getting chips, which motivates Mary to move toward the chips. Once she eats the first chip, this fires off another shot of dopamine that anchors potato chips as a feel-good food, enhancing the dopamine reward feedback loop and strengthening this unhealthy habit (Figure 4). Once that response is anchored, when a stressor causes Mary emotional pain, her subconscious brain will pick potato chips to relieve the pain. This is a habit known as "hedonic eating," when a person uses food as a source of pleasure instead of eating because they're hungry, leading to mindless eating to feel good.[18]

How does our brain determine what it values? It leverages our built-in reward system. Dopamine-producing neurons in the ventral tegmental area communicate with neurons in the nucleus accumbens that assist to evaluate what we like, as well as to motivate us to obtain the things we crave. We can break the reward system with intention, but also by understanding that dopamine is merely a chemical messenger, not a source of lasting pleasure.

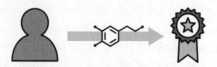

Dopamine is the reward chemical that motivates
us to get on track to get a reward.

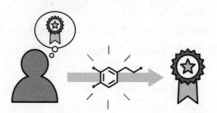

In many cases, anticipating the outcome can increase
dopamine levels that strengthen urge and drive.

FIGURE 4. DOPAMINE REWARD SYSTEM

How Is the Fight-or-Flight System Flawed?

The brain's fight-or-flight system protects us from lethal threats, 24/7. It never turns off, even when we're asleep. An example of how the fight-or-flight system works is when another vehicle comes into your lane while driving down a road. Without any cognitive activity, your fight-or-flight reflex kicks in, and you react to avoid hitting the other vehicle. You immediately take your foot off the gas pedal, pump the brakes, and adjust your steering. Within a millisecond, your cognitive brain catches up, and you may feel a surge of anxiety or relief.

This natural defence system is much needed, even in today's world, where we seldom worry about being eaten by a lion. However, there's an evolutionary flaw. The fight-or-flight system can't clarify the differences between lethal and non-lethal threats. The consequence is whenever we perceive fear, regardless of the type of danger, the fight-or-flight response is activated by the paleomammalian/midbrain (aka caveman brain) that oversees it as well as emotional reactions, automatic thoughts, memory, learning, and appetite regulation.[19] The problem arises when the caveman brain releases chemicals that we don't need. The downside of having fight-or-flight on when we don't need it is that it suppresses the immune system in order to pool all the body's resources to protect it from a lethal threat.

Stress is known to suppress or dysregulate immune function and increase susceptibility to disease.[20] Spending hours each day for weeks and months in a constant state of fear from stress activates the fight-or-flight system and can suppress a person's immune system. Many studies have demonstrated the adverse effects of stress on health.[21]

Our health depends on our autonomic nervous system's ability to balance the sympathetic nervous system (i.e., fight or flight to protect us) and the parasympathetic nervous system. The latter maintains homeostasis, the body's internal monitoring system that ensures everything is working okay, including body temperature and water intake, and helps ensure the body has the energy it needs to work at its optimal level.

Microskills for Managing the Brain's Fight-or-Flight Response

Pay attention to your thoughts. What you think matters. When you start to feel tense and upset, evaluate what you're thinking by asking yourself questions like, "What is it about this situation that's pushing my buttons?" Paying attention to triggers can help you train your brain to not react to non-lethal threats.

Regulate your emotions. Emotional regulation refers to the ability to manage and respond to an emotional experience effectively. If you struggle with emotional outbursts (emotional hijacking that fires off the fight-or-flight response), Cornell researchers Abigail Rolston and Elizabeth Lloyd-Richardson recommend, in addition to critically evaluating the thoughts behind the emotion, staying physically healthy (sleep, diet, and exercise) and doing things each day that give you a sense of achievement so you focus your attention on the positive aspects of your life.[22]

Why Is Becoming Negative Easy?

Negative thinking doesn't happen out of the blue; our subconscious beliefs drive it. What we believe to be true about ourselves and our environment creates our belief system. One challenge is that untruths about ourselves (e.g., "I am...") and others (e.g., "They don't care about me.") that we're not aware of can dominate our belief system. Though we may not be aware of what's in our belief system, it's essential to be clear that we create it based on personal views, attitudes, and values. Adopting self-defeating beliefs contributes to negative thinking, such as that we need to always be perfect, achieve every goal, and be approved of by everyone. Self-defeating thinking results in many personal self-attacks that negatively shape the subconscious beliefs and attitudes about our potential.[23]

It's not hard to become negative, because humans, by design, have a negative bias that causes us to focus more on negative stimuli. The brain is more skilled at noticing and remembering negative experiences than positive ones.[24] This is known as positive-negative asymmetry.[25]

Negative, chronic stress can alter the brain's nervous system, particularly in the limbic system.[26] The brain learns to become negative through repetition. Through neuroplasticity, the way the brain is firing and wiring neurons lays positive or negative tracks.[27] Think about a green field with tall grass. Now picture what happens as you walk back and forth on the same path twenty times. With each pass, the grass lies down and eventually stays down. Similarly, the brain, through repetition, hardwires the most dominant thoughts. It doesn't discriminate between negative and positive. Keep this in mind, because the subconscious brain doesn't evaluate positive or negative beliefs as good or bad; it stores what it's told. If we're aware of what thoughts we allow to run in our head, resist negative ones, and practise being positive, we're more likely to lay positive tracks that support our emotional well-being.

Failing to challenge negative thoughts and accepting them trains the brain to become skewed to negativity. Negative thoughts lower its capacity to work to its full potential.[28] People who fire off more negative than positive thoughts miss many opportunities for creative thinking and struggle more with solving challenging life problems.[29]

Neuroscience has found that we can change our brain's plasticity (i.e., wiring) from predominantly negative to predominantly positive. We do this by adopting positive thinking as a daily practice, through which we can learn to take charge of our brain's health and move from negative to more positive thinking.[30] Neuroscience is finding new evidence that practising to be positive allows old, negative thinking tracks to fade away in favour of positive tracks.[31]

The Reserves ingredient, which you'll learn about in Chapters 13 to 16, involves microskills that promote positive thinking. The following negative thought audit uncovers the link between belief systems and negative thinking. This audit can help you understand that you have a role in how your negative thoughts happen. It's not due to a faulty brain or bad luck.

Negative thought audit

- Situation: What event created the stress trigger that prompted the negative thought?

- Thoughts: What was the first thought that came to mind when you noticed the stress trigger? Was it about you or the situation? Was it positive or negative? Notice if your first thought was negative (e.g., "I deserve...."). If it was, how much do you believe it's true?

- Emotions: What emotions came with this thought—pleasant or unpleasant?

- Physical reaction: What was the reaction in your body (e.g., anxiety, tiredness, headache)?

- Behaviour: What did you do in response to the situation? Did you engage in secure behaviour and confront the situation appropriately, or, being insecure, did you avoid it and isolate yourself?

Belief system reconditioning begins with believing you can influence it. Perform this audit repeatedly until you get the connection and can create the beliefs you want. Your emotional well-being will be shaped by how you manage your brain.

I trust that you have gotten a few valuable insights from this Realization ingredient that you can pay attention to and practise to train your brain to do what you want it to do, rather than allow it to do whatever it wants. The point of this ingredient is to provide you with some fundamental insights into the brain so you can navigate it better—and with any luck, a bit better than your TV remote control.

REFLECTION

- What is your single biggest takeaway from this chapter with respect to supporting emotional well-being?

- What is one thing you can start to practise daily from this chapter that could help you better manage how you react to stress?

Realignment

Intention Can Set the Course for Good Decision Making

The goal is not to be
better than the other man,
but your previous self.

W E WAKE up each day with a choice of how we want to live our life. This may seem like a deep concept, but it really is not as deep so much as it's the truth. How we live our life each day is the result of many microdecisions, whether conscious or unconscious.

We're not robots, with no power to make decisions for ourselves, though it may feel like it some days. Many of us get caught in a mental state similar to autopilot. Once we wake up, we perceive the events of the day are driving what we do. With an autopilot mindset, we're unlikely to notice that we're reacting to the events that unfold each day, rather than living a fulfilling life.

With the ingredient of Realignment, you learn to live each day with focus and intention, ensuring you don't spend your life on autopilot and avoid dealing with current and past regrets. The mindset that you begin each day with will influences how you perceive the world and make decisions in good and challenging times. These decisions affect the number of unpleasant emotions you experience, such as regret or the emotions that arise because of regret, and for how long.

When we don't have a plan for how we live each day, we're prone to be distracted or bumped around by unpleasant emotions. Many of us make about 95 percent of our decisions based on how we feel, not necessarily whether what we're doing is in our best long-term interest.

Deciding to run from unpleasant emotions can have many consequences, such as ending relationships prematurely or quitting something we enjoy. Too often, we make decisions we later regret, or we feel compelled to rationalize them as being correct to protect our ego. Creating a life course for how you choose to live each day is one way to eliminate the guesswork. This section introduces the following:

- The benefits of creating a life plan to approach each day
- How to leverage value-based decision making

8

Locking Down
Your Life Course

WHERE DO you hope to be in five years? This question can be insightful. How you answer it can uncover whether you have a plan or are "winging" it. Do you say, "I will achieve the following outcomes," or, "I think I'll achieve this"? Doing life and living life are two different mindsets.

Doing life is getting up and taking on daily responsibilities with the primary focus on getting through the day. Of course, some of us can be carefree, with no sense of any duties other than what we feel like doing. We each get the choice to create the life we want or to hope for the life we want. Hope is not a plan and can result in living life through reactivity: whatever happens—good or bad—drives our behaviour.

Living life with purpose requires strategy, precise thinking, and a clearly defined life course that sets the discipline for each day. Too many people value the future more than the present. This is unfortunate, because we live in the present, not in the future or the past. Having a defined life course provides certainty about what path we're on. Being aware of what we're doing today influences where we'll be in five years.

Locking down your life course can help ensure you don't miss today, since every day is a gift that can't be taken for granted. When you're caught in the doing-life mode, there's more risk of living on autopilot. Happiness is not a destination; it's a decision from within that what we have now is fulfilling. Think of your life course as a thermostat that helps you regulate your daily level of comfort. Realignment provides you with the awareness to help you make decisions that are aligned with who you want to be, as well to avoid living with any regrets.

Setting your life course is not about perfection; it's about intention. There's a high probability you'll need to adjust it. The global COVID-19 pandemic has taught us that events can create massive disruption in our lives, causing not only severe illness and death but also financial challenges.

Case Study: The Life Partner

Gillian wants nothing more than to find a partner to spend the rest of her life with. She has her career on an upbeat track, enjoys secure friendships, and has a healthy relationship with her family and life passions. What's missing is a safe and healthy life partner. Until being introduced to the ten insights of the Realization ingredient, she didn't know her brain was putting her at a disadvantage. Her constant negative internal dialogue, unpleasant emotions, and anxious attachment have kept her in a state of reactivity and stress. This has led her to train her brain and form a belief system that says she's not loveable or worthy of a life partner. She has no plan to get on track to develop a secure relationship, even though she knows she's a likeable person, based on her workplace and social life experiences. However, she hasn't tried to get the confidence to realize that she can attract or be a worthy life partner. The result is she spends a lot of her free time alone, in mental and emotional churn, filled with unpleasant emotions topped with regret.

The brain insights have opened her eyes to the possibility that she doesn't have to accept her brain's automatic, negative thoughts and old attachment programming. She has the choice and opportunity to reset a new and improved life course with a set of goals and daily actions that build space to learn and heal negative views of herself, so she can feel more emotionally secure and be more attractive to a desirable life partner.

Locking Down Your Life Course

Whether you know it or can define it, your behaviours have set you on some type of life course—planned or reactive. Your habits create the patterns that shape your day, as well as your emotional well-being. Locking down your life course begins with being honest with yourself. It's never too late to improve your life, provided you have the desire. All that's required is motivation.

Wanting more is a common plight, but getting more rarely equals happiness. It's called mis-wanting. Many people have discovered firsthand how more money, more cars, and more nice clothes don't equal happiness. This faulty thinking of wanting more can explain why some people don't believe they can be happy until they get XYZ. True happiness doesn't come from getting more. It comes from within, knowing we're living in a way that we're personally satisfied with— and that can only come from within.

In the end, nothing makes us happy other than deciding that we're satisfied with what we have. We can only do that when we're awake and focusing on our emotional well-being, rooted in how we manage our daily thoughts and emotions. There's nothing wrong with wanting to achieve a life goal. The missed opportunity for too many is when we don't allow ourselves to enjoy today until we get what we think we need to be happy.

REFLECTION

- On a scale of 1 (low) to 5 (high), how confident are you that you have locked down your life course and are living it?

- You can adjust your life course to adapt to changing wants and needs. People living with purpose are more dynamic and open to constantly learning how to improve their day-to-day experience.

- If you're unsure if you're on your life course, that's okay; in fact, it's standard. However, every day you live without a life course, you risk making decisions that negatively influence your emotional well-being.

- The purpose of realignment is to help you become the person you want to be rather than getting caught up thinking about who you wish you were. This ingredient is a powerful antidote for living a life with no regrets.

Positive Mental Fitness

In *The Cure for Loneliness,* I introduced my algorithm for mental health.[1] It includes environmental supports (e.g., social determinants of health), physical health, social connections, and mental fitness (e.g., engaging in pro-health behaviours and decision making). This algorithm suggests that having good mental health requires the knowledge and skills to make healthy life decisions. One pillar for positive mental fitness is intentionally engaging in prosocial behaviour: any healthy behaviour that charges our mental battery, is enjoyable, is good for mental health, and doesn't hurt anyone in any way.

Locking down a life course is a robust prosocial behaviour for emotional well-being. It lays out a daily road map for living and making healthy decisions about experiences, thoughts, and emotions and focuses on what matters.

Not having a locked-down life course is why people like Gillian can feel regret about parts of their life. To the onlooker, she appeared to have things together. However, she felt lost and incomplete, living in a constant state of regret. Locking down your life course creates your passport to emotional well-being. Peace and happiness are the most valuable assets we can obtain for emotional well-being. When they're in place, everything in life appears better.

9

Designing Your Life Course

WHAT DOES an artist do before they start to paint? They tap into their inspiration and vision. Most do this before they touch a brush to canvas. While they can develop their thinking and make changes as they paint, they've already decided whether they're painting the sky at night or day.

Living with eyes only on the future is a common human mistake because this mindset puts less value on the joys of today. Locking down a life course is about living each day to its fullest so you can arrive at an endpoint in life emotionally satisfied and with little risk of experiencing regrets. Regardless of what we've painted in our life to this point, we can't change the past. However, it's our painting, and we get to decide what we want to keep, change, or do differently. It's never too late. While we still have breath, we can choose to improve our emotional well-being.

The Five Core Pillars Inventory

Before locking down your life course, complete the following Five Core Pillars inventory. Each pillar is worthy of reflection on its own merit. On a scale of 1 (low) to 5 (high), evaluate the level of confidence you have in each pillar. It's essential to do this inventory without judgement; it's too easy to be critical. Just notice what you think and feel for each pillar.

1 **Purpose:** I'm clear on why I get up each day. ____

2 **Vision:** I'm clear on who I want to be. ____

3 **Values:** I'm clear on what's most important to me, and what influences my daily decisions. ____

4 **Wants:** I'm clear on what I want in my personal and professional lives. ____

5 **Boundaries:** I'm clear on what boundaries I will set for my personal (e.g., emotional, sexual, financial) and professional (e.g., ethical, ability to plug out) lives. ____

Any one of these pillars, if ignored, can explain why you may feel unsure about where you are in your life journey. The underpinning factor for locking down your life course is establishing that you don't have to be like a leaf constantly blown around by every gust of wind (e.g., life challenges).

Case Study: Lack of Motivation

Devasted about losing his job, Jake, an educated forty-four-year-old, booked an appointment to see me. He believed he'd lost his job because of his stupidity. As Jake unpacked his story, he shared that he hadn't done his best work each day because of his lack of motivation. He believed that if he had tried harder, he would still have his job. He was grieving the loss and regretting not having done better at work.

After listening to Jake unpack his story for about twenty minutes, I asked him one question that appeared to surprise him. "Why do you think you weren't motivated to do your job?"

Without missing a beat, Jake said it was because he found his job boring and unfulfilling. This response was the door to move us away from regret and to start discussing his life course. It wasn't that he lacked motivation in general—just for this particular job.

People like Jake come to see mental health professionals when they're struggling because they feel life is challenging and overwhelming. They typically want some support to cope better. Sometimes, we can feel a sense of regret over a relationship or situation that's not healthy or good for us. One significant benefit to locking down your life course is committing to making conscious decisions to live each day with intention and purpose.

Framing Your Life Course as a Daily Focus

This activity aims to make the five core pillars part of your daily routine. When you live by these pillars, you're living with intention that sets you on a course to become the person you want to be.

Mission 1: Exploring the Five Core Pillars

Without spending much mental energy, quickly go through the following list. For each pillar, write down the first thought that comes to your mind. Then, evaluate your level of satisfaction with each response on a scale of 1 (low) to 10 (high). This brainstorming can help bring to your attention what you're doing with intention and what gaps you will benefit from closing. The more aware you are of each pillar, the more awake you are.

Purpose: Why I get up each day

_____

_____

Satisfaction: ____

Vision: How I want my life to go

_____

_____

Satisfaction: ____

Values: What is most important to me

_____

_____

Satisfaction: ____

Wants: What I want in my personal and professional lives

_____

_____

Satisfaction: ____

Boundaries: What boundaries I have in place in my personal and professional lives

_____

_____

Satisfaction: ____

Mission 2: Shaping your Five Core Pillars

In Mission 1, you brought ideas to the surface and evaluated your satisfaction with how you're practising these ideas daily. Mission 2 will shape what you want your pillars to be. Be specific. Complete each sentence, then, on a scale of 1 (low) to 10 (high), rate how confident you are today that you are focused on what you have written and are living it daily. The confidence score establishes your baseline so that you can dial in on areas you can improve.

You can adjust your pillar definitions if you feel there is a need. Your priorities may change due to life circumstances, and you may want to renew or rethink what is important in any one of the five pillars. Since you have only so much energy, the rationale for locking down your core pillars is to begin by deciding how you want to live each day and who you want to be.

My life **purpose** is

_____

_____

Confidence: ____

My life **vision** is

_____

_____

_____

_____

Confidence: ____

My top three core **values** are

1 _____

2 _____

3 _____

Confidence: ____

My top two **wants** for my personal life are

1 _____

2 _____

Confidence: ____

My top two **wants** for my professional life are

1 _____

2 _____

Confidence: ____

My top two **boundaries** for my personal life are

1 _____

2 _____

Confidence: ____

My top two **boundaries** for my professional life are

1 _____

2 _____

Confidence: ____

Mission 3: Setting Your Daily Focus

The overall mission for this ingredient is for your five core pillars to become daily habits. It may take you weeks or months to get to the point where you're aligned with your pillars without having to do much thinking. Reaching that point is a process, not just something you decide to do. Choosing to lock down your life course is critical, as is focusing on it and installing it into your daily life.

Focusing generates attention, which is a powerful motivator for putting energy into the area of our life we want to learn how to live to its fullest.[1] Installing a core pillar may require new knowledge and skills, such as learning what boundaries are or how to set them. A boundary is anything that happens that you don't want to talk about. Boundaries in personal relationships can be emotional, financial, related to communications, sexual, and time-based. Under each, there may be specific expectations you want to have in place to feel psychologically safe. If you have a career and work, you'll benefit by being clear on your boundaries regarding work demand, communications, and when you'll plug in and plug out. The first step is to name the boundary, followed by defining and implementing it by informing the people who need to know. Then it's up to you to enforce your limit.

It's also up to you to determine whether you need some support or training to help you explore each of the pillars. Brainstorming with a trusted person or working with a coach can help you make decisions and formulate focus areas. Thinking about your core life pillars is an important step, as is practising them daily. Research suggests that setting a daily focus can drive the life experiences we want each day.[2] A fulfilling life is not about how much we can cram into each day; it's living each day with a sense of purpose. Focusing on a couple of things creates a mental state for learning and habit formation.

You're the only person who can lock down your life course until it becomes a habit. Willpower is not a long-term strategy, but it can help get you on track. Be patient and accept that it will take time to lock down your five core pillars to the point where they're habits. If you find yourself becoming frustrated, leveraging the other ingredients in this book can increase your ability to tolerate frustration.

When setting your focus areas, set clear timelines for how long you expect it will take to get some aspect of a pillar in place. For example, it may take thirty days to establish your workplace boundaries. Also, keep in mind the *why* as you do this: for your five core pillars to become the filters through which you make decisions.

PERSONAL FOCUS AREA

Targeted pillar: _____

Desired outcome:

_____

_____

Start date: _____

Action steps to obtain desired outcome:

_____

_____

What success looks like:

_____

_____

End date: _____

PROFESSIONAL FOCUS AREA

Targeted pillar: _____

Desired outcome:

_____

_____

Start date: _____

Action steps to obtain desired outcome:

_____

_____

What success looks like:

_____

_____

End date: _____

Mission 4: Five Core Pillars Daily Log

Keeping a daily log that will help with attention and personal accountability can help to install new habits and maintain them. By taking a few moments at the end of the day, you can honestly and objectively evaluate and recognize what you did well and what you can do better. I find daily logs and reflections at the start and end of the day a wonderful ritual for an objective, honest measurement of how congruent I am with my life course. It's not about being perfect; it's about trying to become as close to the person we really want to be so that we don't end up regretting that we didn't do all we could.

You may have days that feel hard, when you become distracted and lose your focus. That's okay. Losing your focus has nothing to do with being weak or strong. Getting back on track requires a little self-compassion, so take a deep breath and refocus.

The magic of attention and focus is they can help you get your core life pillars in place to assist in maturing your emotional well-being. When it comes to creating alignment with how we want to live our life, we can learn from the wisdom of one of the great teachers, the Dalai Lama. He promotes the benefit of being clear on who we want to be, why we want to be this person, and how we can live with intention daily. Emotional well-being comes from within; there are no magic shots or pills for it. Finding it involves accepting that life is not perfect, nor should we expect it to be. All we can count on is what we choose to do each day. It's no more complicated than that.

To help with alignment, I've provided an example of a framework for monitoring daily focus areas (both personal and professional) and pausing to see how well you are doing with living the five pillars. The purpose is to take conversations out of your head and put them on paper. Writing out your reflections can help you discover, create accountability, and release emotions. After many years of clinical work, one human flaw I have noticed is that when we feel good, we stop doing what helped us get to that point. I am a big fan of daily reflection and journaling and personally find the model below helpful. Of course, you can free journal or build a template like mine.

Sample Five Core Pillars Daily Log

FOCUS AREAS
Personal: Emotional reactivity to stress

Level of confidence I was focused on this area today (1 to 10): 7

What I'm most satisfied with today regarding this focus area: I caught myself emotionally reacting to my partner and quickly apologized. It was short, and that is aligned with my desire to be a loving partner.

How I can improve this focus area tomorrow: Continue practising observing that unpleasant emotions are just chemicals that do not control me. When my partner gives me feedback when I am tired, I have a choice. I do not have to react. I can take five and find calm before responding.

Professional:

FIVE PILLARS
Reflections on how living by each factor is adding value to my emotional well-being

Purpose: I woke up feeling pride and purpose in my family and work super-charged.

Level of confidence I lived congruent with this factor today (1 to 10): 9

Vision: Today I lived my life on the right path to get me where I want to be.

Level of confidence I lived congruent with this factor today (1 to 10): 8

Values: I lived my values today and showed up how I want to.

Level of confidence I lived congruent with this factor today (1 to 10): 9

Wants: I focused well on being a loving partner and meeting my clients' needs. I know I can do better with my partner. I want to keep this a focus as I never want them to believe I take them for granted or do not care.

Level of confidence I lived congruent with this factor today (1 to 10): 7

Boundaries: I said no to an extra assignment to ensure I was home on time for supper with family.

Level of confidence I lived congruent with this factor today (1 to 10): 10

Reputation

Daily Choices Influence What We and Others Believe to Be True

Nothing can dim the light
which shines from within.

MAYA ANGELOU

ONCE HAD a client say to me, "If it were not for how I feel, I could be happy." If you process this line for a moment, a few questions may come to mind. Mine was, "What do you feel?" Their response: "Nothing good." The truth is, they were feeling, but not feeling what they wanted. How we deal with our feelings may be one of the most important life skills to master if we want emotional well-being. Few get any training, and perhaps that's why mental illness is becoming a leading cause of premature death. People are becoming stuck in unpleasant emotions that are affecting how they experience the world.

You can meditate for hours a day and still experience unpleasant emotions, which are chemicals triggered by a perceived or real threat. They alter how we feel and grab our attention but don't tell us how to respond; we decide that. If we have trained our brain that unpleasant chemicals are bad, this can create unhealthy coping habits, such as avoidance and acting out, that seldom make the situation any better.

A key point for maturing our emotional well-being is to own that we are accountable for how we manage our unpleasant emotions and how we show up under pressure. Some of us are better at dealing with emotions. It could be due to parenting, community support, mentors, teachers, coaches, therapy, training, genetics, or practice. It doesn't matter where we are today or what we have done. We can't change any of this. All we can change is what we choose to do and how we decide to show up now and in the future.

When we make decisions that are not aligned with who we want to be, it can result in regret. When we take the time to be clear on who we want to be and how we want to show up each day, we can increase our self-awareness and personal accountability to become the person we really want to be through action. Thoughts do not create a life of no regrets; intentional actions do.

Key topics covered in this ingredient are the following:

- How our personal brand affects how others see us and whether they want to spend time with us

- How to develop emotional literacy (i.e., navigate unpleasant emotions and create pleasant emotions on demand)

- Microskills for managing unpleasant emotions

10

Showing Up as the Person You Want to Be

Y OUR BEHAVIOUR shapes what others think about your reputation—the overall qualities or character as seen or judged by people in general.[1] Personal and professional contexts define reputation. When reputation is negatively affected by reactive decisions or lack of awareness, this can result in social rejection, which can trigger regret.

Ultimately, the two audiences that define your reputation are the people within your personal and professional universes and you. What you think about your reputation may differ from what others think, particularly if you're not keen or objective or don't care to consider others' perspectives. For example, if you're aggressive and not aware of (or don't care) how your behaviour impacts others, you'll likely develop a reputation as an aggressive person.

Reputations are hard to change because we tend to hold on to negative experiences with more conviction than positive experiences. People are motivated by pain and pleasure. When interacting with you is more painful than pleasant, this influences how you're perceived and drives how much others value you or want to be around you. Once a person forms a negative perception of you, there's nothing you can do other than focus on what's in your control. You can't talk yourself into having a good reputation; you can only behave your way into it.

One common regret many have is not getting along with people they care about. Why does this happen? There are many reasons. One is not paying enough attention to how your behaviour is affecting their experience with you. Every interaction with you is an opportunity for a positive or negative experience. These experiences collectively influence what others think about you. Reputation is the filter through which people see you and define your value to them. Being considered kind is much more beneficial for building relationships than being viewed as a bully.

Building a positive reputation is jeopardized when we allow our ego to get in the way. Ego doesn't care about what others think; it only cares about self. Ego pushes some to focus on worldly things and appearances, such as the clothes worn, car driven, and club attended. These people believe that obtaining status and material things will enhance their reputation more than deepening meaningful, authentic relationships. Humility is the antidote to ego. It's not an initiative; it's a learned skill.

What you choose to do in every interaction influences your reputation and personal brand—how others see you and describe you. Amazon CEO Jeff Bezos says, "Your brand is what people say about you when you're not in the room."[2]

Being Mindful of How You Show Up Each Day

Do you pay attention to how you show up each day? You may be surprised how many people don't because they're too focused on their emotions or what they want. Ego cares only about getting what it thinks it deserves, not what's fair or rational. Why? Because its sole role is making you feel important. When not managed, your ego can hurt your reputation. Knowing how to tame it is critical for building your brand.

The benefit of learning to tame your ego's constant demands is developing more internal calm and satisfaction, which aid your mental state and emotional well-being. By developing your emotional literacy, you can prevent unpleasant emotions from driving reactivity that fuels defensiveness and winning at all costs. Calmly managing unpleasant emotions can position your ego to be open to feedback that will shape your reputation.

Deciding to be more aware of your ego creates space to care about how you show up. Showing up is not about being perfect; it's accepting that others have emotions, wants, and needs that may be different than yours, and this is not a bad thing. Showing up healthily aids your reputation by building respectful interactions and relationships.

Considerations that influence how you show up:

- **Positive mindset:** It's impossible to have 100 percent positive thoughts, but the more you have about yourself and others, the better. Paying attention to what you say to yourself and think about others matters because it programs your belief system.

- **Calm under pressure:** Negative emotions can spark fear. However, when there's no lethal threat, you can notice your emotions and be curious about what triggered them. Just as a positive emotion doesn't mean you need to feel out of control, yelling because you're happy, a negative emotion doesn't require any different intensity than noticing it with a commitment to remain calm so you can focus energy on your response.

- **Security:** The more secure you are with your thoughts and emotions, the more likely you can respond with a sense of security. A non-secure response focuses on the self, resulting in being defensive or making a judgement about another person. A secure response focuses on the other person and looks past the negative emotion to understand their position. The goal is to allow them to feel heard and understood.

REFLECTION

What do you believe is your brand? Use the following list as a guide to think about what you imagine others feel about you based on how you believe you show up each day:

- I do what I say.
- I'm loyal.
- I'm honest.
- I'm a hard worker.
- I'm caring.
- I'm confident.

List what you think are the top three qualities that others would say define your brand. The purpose of this reflection is to check in on your ego. Test your list with three trusted sources. If you discover a blind spot from the feedback, look at it as a found gem and an opportunity to provide your ego with more direction and guidance.

Every interaction you have with a person or group is an opportunity to strengthen or weaken your brand. Others perceive things as true about you from their direct experiences with you or what they've heard others have experienced.

Be Nice; It Matters!

When we're hyper-focused on what we want, we may miss opportunities to be nice to other people. Being nice begins with being mindful of how our actions can have a positive or negative impact. Walking by someone without acknowledging them may be perceived as not being nice. Not noticing them because we're distracted may sound like a reasonable excuse. But is it? Intention doesn't matter; what matters is the other person's experience.

Being nice is not only what we do but also what we think. When we see peers at work, we may have no idea what's happening in their lives—how much fear or stress they may be dealing with. When we're absorbed in our reality and ignore others, we miss opportunities to ease their strain. We also can be adding to it by our actions. If we want to create more civility in the workplace, it's important to accept that not paying attention to our behaviours and how they're received increases our risk of being rude and dismissive of others. Consider how dismissive we can be if we allow ourselves to assume that the way we're operating is just fine. By not acknowledging others and not being nice, we may be creating barriers instead of knocking them down.

Most people have a frame of reference of "nice." When we're nice, we're intentionally pleasing, agreeable, and delightful. We're not necessarily doing anything such as overt acts of kindness. We're just creating positive energy that's safe for another person. Being judgemental, sarcastic, or rude is the opposite of nice.

Microskills for Being Nice

Do a self-evaluation. Being nice often starts with being mindful of what we're doing. On a scale of 1 (not very nice at all) to 5 (very nice all the time), rate how your average peer, employee, and family member would score you. Next, ask two trusted sources how they would score you. Being open to the possibility we have blind spots and being willing to learn from them influences personal growth.

Be consistent. Some people save their nice factor for those they value. This isn't being nice. Being nice to everyone can positively frame your mood, which is good for mental health. It can also provide positive energy and support to the people you meet. People like being around nice people. It doesn't take a lot to be nice to others. However, it does require awareness, intention, and deciding to be nice. Those seen as being nice often are perceived as more influential and valued. They don't need to take a course; they need only choose to be nice.

Be tolerant. Accept that being nice doesn't always mean you're going to get nice back. Knowing this can help create the expectation that you don't need to match another person who may not being nice in return, intentionally or unintentionally. One challenge with interacting with people is we all have stuff running in our heads. How we manage what's happening in our world influences how we behave to others. It's wise not to take things personally and to accept that there's a high probability that another person's not being nice has nothing to do with you.

Be intentional. Being nice requires self-awareness and desire. I can recall having clients on Wall Street write the words "Be Nice" on the top of their notepads to remind them to be nice when interacting with junior staff. This simple act built trust and created a culture where junior bankers felt supported and encouraged by their leaders rather than flawed or weak—a critical factor in determining whether they described their supervisor as a psychologically safe leader.

11

Emotions Matter

MAINTAINING EMOTIONAL composure during challenging moments is a learned skill. When we overreact to a situation, it can create hardship and strained or even broken relationships. This can result in regret. How confident are you that you can manage your emotions under pressure? Your brand and emotional well-being are influenced by how well you manage your emotions. The Reputation ingredient can help you learn to not overreact when faced with a challenge and filled with unpleasant emotion. It is difficult to show up and be the person we want to be when we feel powerless to cope with unpleasant emotions like regret. By developing skills to better navigate emotions, we are more able to take control of life situations in a way that meets our reputational needs.

Unpleasant emotions can influence how you feel, but the more you develop your emotional literacy, the more likely you'll feel you have control over your emotions, and the better able you'll be to control your mood, which determines how you show up. The Oji Emotions Life Lab provides distinctions between emotions, feelings, and mood:[1]

- Emotions: short-lived responses to stimuli (either real or imagined) that cause a shift in reasoning, physiological expression, and behaviour.

- Feelings: the short-term, private experiences of emotions. They're often more complex and can represent a mixture of several emotions at once. Love and shame are examples.

- Moods: emotional states that may have an identifiable cause, last longer, and are less intense than the experience of a singular emotion.

According to the Oji Emotions Life Lab, there could be up to 2,193 emotions, something I find overwhelming to believe because I can barely name a hundred.[2] Regardless of how many, they will happen and impact our mood, which influences our energy levels and how we show up. Being aware of and monitoring our mood is a choice. As Norman Vincent Peale, the author of *The Power of Positive Thinking*, taught, we each have the daily choice to put energy toward positive thoughts if we want to feel better.[3]

Unpleasant emotions come from a fear originating from some threat that can be real or perceived. The way we react to and cope with these experiences influences our mood and shapes our overall emotional well-being. People who spend a large percentage of their day in unpleasant emotions like languishing experience strained emotional well-being. In a *New York Times* article, Adam Grant wrote that many people struggled during COVID-19 because of languishing, which is a state of feeling stagnant and empty.[4] Grant suggested that languishing is an emotional state between depression and flourishing, defined as the absence of wellness. A person caught in languishing doesn't have a mental illness; however, the longer they're in this emotional state, the higher their risk of mental illness and addictions.

Emotional Literacy

Emotional literacy is a skill that I'm not convinced is mainstream, like reading and writing. Why? It's not yet a part of the education system curriculum as a critical life skill. The result is that a large percentage of adults don't know how to manage their emotions or cope with unpleasant emotions. Many run from them or try to numb them. Emotions create urges that drive most human behaviour. I often say in my keynotes, "We humans would like to think we're rational creatures, but we're not. We're often too sensitive and emotional." Now, you can agree or disagree with my statement. However, ask yourself this: From your experiences, how confident are you that you can healthily manage unpleasant emotions?

Emotional literacy is the degree to which we can identify and manage all kinds of emotions, a skill we can learn at any age, provided we see the benefit and are motivated. With this skill, we're much less likely to react to unpleasant emotions and make kneejerk decisions we'll later regret. When you hear bad news that upsets you, there's no menu for you to pick which emotion you'll feel. In less than a second, your brain, based on the perceived context and subconscious belief system, fires off one or more emotions related to your circumstances.

Whether a pleasant or unpleasant emotion pops up is not the concern. It's what you do with it that is of concern. Unpleasant emotions are not evil; they're transient emotions that come and go, just like pleasant emotions. For emotional well-being, it's necessary to understand and discover that we'll not always be living in pleasant emotions, nor do we need to be. Instead of fighting, hiding, or running from unpleasant emotions like regret, learn how to observe them for what they are: information, nothing more. There's no need to react to them.

Emotional literacy teaches that when emotions arise, we don't have to accept them or react to them, because they're based on perceptions that our mental state can influence, not always on facts. For example, in a negative state, we're more likely to experience a situation as negative and attach more negative emotions to it. If we have emotional literacy, we can notice the negative emotions, become curious about what's behind them, and decide how we want to behave. The way we manage unpleasant emotions influences how we experience the world and our brand. When one part of our life that's upsetting us spills over and negatively affects another area, this can create strain on other people who are not directly involved. Developing emotional literacy can help us create a sense of control and learn to not fear or overreact to unpleasant emotions.

REFLECTION

Emotional literacy is how aware we are of emotions. It can teach us how to connect mind and body better. Unpleasant emotions create headaches, fatigue, nausea, tension, worry, stiffness, and dizziness. Positive emotions can generate a sense of glowing, feeling excited, and charged with energy.

* What emotion are you experiencing now?

* If you're unsure, it's okay. Repeat this question five times a day over the next week. One way to do this is to set your alarm to trigger this question every two hours. If you keep coming up with a blank after one week or can't be in touch with your emotions, this a sign for you to dig into emotional literacy.

Emotional Regulation

I listened to a MasterClass by Chris Voss, a world-famous hostage negotiator.[5] He made two comments that got me thinking: in a positive mental state, we're 31 percent smarter; in a negative state, 31 percent dumber. This assessment caught my attention, as I happen to believe it's true. I look at all the personal challenges I've had with my children over the years, and most of them were because I was caught in unpleasant emotions and often didn't say or do what I would have in a calm state. How I know this is I had to go back more than once to apologize and try another approach. My knee-jerk, reactive parenting was never as effective as my calm and thoughtful parenting. Whenever those who are not aware of emotional literacy experience a difference between what they want and what they have, they're prone to emotional reactivity—kneejerk reactions to escape or stop the unpleasant emotion as quickly as possible.

Emotional regulation is a common skills gap for those who haven't developed their emotional literacy and are prone to overreacting to unpleasant emotions. They're at risk of engaging in maladaptive coping skills (at-risk behaviours) such as substance use, suicidal ideation, impulsivity, self-injury, and acting-out behaviour, referred to as emotional dysregulation, the inability to control or regulate emotional responses healthily.[6] Developing emotional literacy provides an opportunity for experiencing unpleasant emotions with less reactivity, emotion, and mental pain. We can't control or prevent all the stress, life challenges, and hardships we will face in the future. However, the more we discover and practise developing emotional literacy, the better we'll become at coping and living with unpleasant emotions.

Emotions play an essential role in how well we function and perform. Dr. Marc Brackett, from the Yale Center for Emotional Intelligence, teaches that emotions influence

- attention, memory, and learning;
- decision making;
- relationships;
- physical and mental health; and
- creativity and performance.[7]

We have all observed at least one situation where a person who reacted emotionally and engaged in some kneejerk reaction (e.g., anger) ended up with a negative outcome that they could have avoided. Learning to monitor our emotions and regulate unpleasant ones is a must for finding peace of mind. I have a diabetic friend whom I care deeply about. Whenever we're golfing, I find myself asking them several times, "How are your sugar and insulin levels? Are they okay?" They appreciate that I care and often check their monitor when I ask and say, "Thanks for asking; all looks okay," or they take any required action to adjust their levels. Monitoring sugar and insulin levels to protect their physical health is not an option for them—it's a must.

Emotional regulation is a skill that can assist in coping better with unpleasant emotions like rejection, worry, excitement, frustration, anxiety, and feeling low. Many unpleasant emotions result from direct interaction with another human, replaying a historical event, worrying about a future event, or being unhappy with what's happening now. Emotional regulation is training the brain to not overreact to, or fear, unpleasant emotions. Avoiding them altogether can have a negative impact on a relationship.

I invite you to try the ERP (expect, resist, pivot) mnemonic I've created to help me navigate unpleasant emotions.

It will install a strategy that, with practice, can become a positive habit. By repeatedly focusing on learning this model, you'll learn how to avoid reacting to unpleasant emotions and influence your emotions in a healthy way, rather than feeling trapped. To learn ERP, I suggest running it through your head four or five times a day. Don't expect perfection or that you'll develop this skill overnight. It can take several months to master emotional regulation. Accepting awareness and accountability for your emotions, thoughts, and behaviours is an excellent place to start.

ERP helps you become aware that you can rewire how your brain responds to stimuli or threats. You can train your brain so that it doesn't need to jump and react to unpleasant emotions. Instead of feeling an urge to avoid, you can lean into unpleasant emotions and change your perspective by focusing on the situation, not on yourself. When you can recognize that a situation is neither good nor bad but just a situation, you'll be open to the fact that others involved have emotions, and your response can influence them positively or negatively. It comes down to deciding how you want to show up for yourself and others by managing your emotions.

ERP Mnemonic for Emotional Regulation

Expect unpleasant emotions. Prepare for unpleasant emotions by acknowledging there's no removing them.

- Accept that unpleasant emotions will pop up without notice.

- Understand that unpleasant emotions are nothing more than the brain sending a signal for action.

- Emotions create urges. They don't control behaviour choices; they only influence the need to act. We get to choose how we act and what we will ignore.

- Accept that regardless of unpleasant emotions, all behaviours and decisions are ours.

Resist reacting. Once you notice an unpleasant emotion, name it.

- If you feel an urge to act, put your foot on the reaction brake pedal. Give yourself time for your conscious brain to catch up by training it to run the following script: "Something doesn't feel good right now. Okay, step back and get all the facts; don't react."

- As you practise resisting the urge to act, you'll develop the ability to tolerate unpleasant emotions rather than trying to avoid or fight them.

- Do all you can to resist the urge to act impulsively, as this often creates more emotional churn and strain.

- Recognize the situation for what it is, not what it feels like.

- Question what thoughts are connected to the unpleasant emotion.

- Become an emotional engineer and understand that unpleasant emotions don't mean a situation is terrible; it's just uncomfortable for a reason. Allow yourself to look for ways that you can best deal with the situation.

Pivot toward a pleasant emotion. Pay attention to others and the kind of emotions they're projecting.

- Focus on the other people involved. Notice what emotions they're experiencing.

- Focus on the situation and the outcome you want. Notice how this can drive cognitive activity that can help you move out of emotional reactivity.

- Determine what kind of emotions are most appropriate for the situation (e.g. being calm and collaborative will facilitate a better outcome than rage).

- Challenge the unpleasant emotion's value and focus on a better emotion.

- Initiate the desired emotion and put some energy into it.

- Keep the focus on the situation, and don't fight unpleasant emotions; give your attention to the desired outcome.

ERP is a framework that requires your willingness to practise it. When I showed this model to a fantastic person with lots of passion and purpose but who lived their life in constant upset when I first met them, they asked, "How long will it take to master it?" I said without hesitation, "For you, three years." They questioned, "What? Three years?" I responded, "Correct, you said 'to master.' But to get some benefit, give yourself three months and allow for some slips to old habits. This will take you some time. If you want to learn to be more composed and less reactive, you can if you make the effort. When you overreact, you'll know it, and you can apologize and commit to doing better the next time." They smiled and accepted that they owned it, and it would take time and intention. I've found that setting focused and realistic expectations and understanding change is a process. When it comes to emotional well-being, there are no magic pills.

If you don't believe you can learn to regulate your emotions on your own, meet with a mental health professional for guidance. Avoiding your emotions will only make life harder and put you at greater risk of living life with regrets.

Plan to Improve Emotional Regulation

The ERP framework may appear simple, but it takes effort and self-compassion to master. If you struggle with your emotions and find you're constantly getting upset, it will take some time to learn how to shift.

Mission 1: Emotional Regulation Debriefing

Leveraging the ERP mnemonic, I've found practising emotional regulation debriefing helpful. Instead of regretting an emotional slip, we can focus our energy next time. Review the statements below and consider whether you believe each to be true. Is your response "No" or a confident "Yes"?

- Pleasant mood: I have a choice in setting my mood for the day.

- Calm under pressure: I have a choice about how I respond emotionally.

- Secure response: I have a choice about how I respond under pressure.

Mastering the ability to regulate unpleasant emotions requires practice, self-reflection, and honest self-appraisal. The more you practise with intention, the more likely you'll learn how to cope better with unpleasant emotions so that you become more aware and comfortable and, when needed, tolerant of them, rather than trying to run from them.

Mission 2: Putting ERP into Action

This mission is about applying ERP to your day-to-day life to reduce your risk of being overtaken by unpleasant emotions. Emotions are powerful, and we can quickly get lost in them.

The good news is the more we're mindful and start to examine our reactions, behaviours, and choices and accept that we can learn to regulate unpleasant emotions better, the more we can learn to do better. As we're developing our emotional literacy, it's essential to resist reacting to the first thoughts that pop into our head as true or the only choices we have. Regardless of what we feel, we're always accountable for our behaviour.

A secure response refers to a mature and thoughtful action (e.g., considers other emotions). A non-secure response is focused only on the individual's wants and emotions. In this highly charged, unpleasant emotional state, they're more likely to focus on how hard things are for them, with no regard for the other person. They say mean things and are judgemental. A secure response is being calm and mindful of the other person's emotions, not judgemental. The more we can respond securely and be less focused on our own emotions, the more we'll be perceived by others as stable and calm under pressure, which will support our emotional well-being and promote a positive brand.

ON-DEMAND EMOTIONAL DEBRIEFING LOG
Use this debriefing log to help you develop your ERP skill.

Date: _____

Personal or professional situation:

_____

Emotional event (high level, brief overview):

_____

_____

_____

_____

People involved: ____

SUMMARY OF YOUR EMOTIONAL RESPONSE
Notice how the factors affecting your emotional response can fluctuate. The higher you can get your percentage of emotional response to be positive, calm, and secure, the more successful you'll be at managing unpleasant emotions under pressure.

Mindset: ____% positive ____% negative

State under pressure: ____% calm ____% upset

Security of response: ____% secure ____% non-secure

Outcome:

_____

_____

For next time, I will:

_____

_____

12

Initiating Emotions

W E CAN learn to initiate pleasant (positive) emotions through practice. This is a powerful tool to have to be able to move away from unpleasant emotions like regret on demand. This skill, when practised and developed, can support us by prompting us to pay attention to the quality of the questions we ask ourselves—the ones that influence our attention and decisions. If an unpleasant emotion is distracting you, notice the questions running in your head, such as, "How did this happen?" "Why is this happening?" These questions focus your mind on the unpleasant emotion.

If something happened in your life that you didn't want to happen and you keep asking yourself why it did, it becomes your primary focus. It creates an emotional, negative feedback loop that generates an endless abundance of unpleasant emotions that don't serve your emotional well-being. Unpleasant emotions have their purpose, but when they hold you in a constant state of churn that strains your emotional well-being, they're not helpful.

By asking yourself questions that challenge unpleasant emotions, however, you position yourself to change your focus. When it comes to any emotion, what you focus on will expand. You can release an unpleasant emotion by asking questions like, "Is focusing on this situation and feeling the way I do serving my higher emotional well-being?" The answer is no. You can initiate pleasant emotions by changing your attention to something you enjoy and find positive. Where you direct your focus and energy, your emotions will follow.

REFLECTION

- Create a positive emotion generation list. List twenty things you enjoy doing that generate positive, pleasant emotions such as joy, happiness, fun, and calmness. These should be activities that are within your control. Building your list provides you with a preplanned set of activities you can engage in to initiate pleasant emotions.

- Some examples: playing with your pet, golfing, running, enjoying a comedy, calling a friend, walking, boating, skiing, working at your hobby, visiting family, travelling, volunteering, writing, gardening, reading, meditating, watching a movie, going to the gym, watching sports, playing a sport, eating out, visiting friends.

Focusing on what we want to do changes our attention and puts us in a position to initiate more desirable and helpful feelings. Many of us, by habit, default to focusing on what we don't like or have that brings up unpleasant emotions. We'll never stop this, but we can notice when it's happening, seek to understand if there's anything useful we can learn from these emotions, and then change our focus. Knowledge is not helpful unless we act on it. By becoming an emotional engineer, we notice our emotions and accept that we have free will and the ability to tolerate unpleasant emotions and, when desired, initiate pleasant emotions.

Of course, some people take this positive emotion stuff to an extreme, which is known as positivity toxicity. This is where, no matter how serious or challenged the person's belief, it's important for them to be constantly projecting a positive attitude to others.[1] This isn't a healthy approach, as it results in stuffing down and avoiding emotions without dealing with them. Failing to acknowledge hardships can negatively affect our mental health.[2] Emotional literacy is not about running from unpleasant emotions. It's about noticing them, learning from them, and asking better questions to initiate more pleasant feelings. Those who have high emotional literacy also know they'll never be happy all the time, nor do they need to be. However, focusing on developing emotional literacy can help them achieve more favourable outcomes.

Focus on Subjective Wellness First

Research suggests that happiness is a set of skills we can learn through practice. Fifty percent of happiness is genetic, 10 percent is based on the environment, and 40 percent is a result of what we do.[3] This implies that if we want more happiness, we need to understand that we have a significant role in creating it, independent of our life circumstances.

Harvard professor Arthur Brooks, in his article in the *Atlantic* "The 3 Equations for a Happy Life, Even During a

Pandemic," provides an illuminating summary of what he describes as the equations that define our sense of happiness.[4] What is fantastic to me is that most of us are trying to find happiness without having a compass to tell us where to point. We have the option of setting our true north to default on negativity or focusing more on initiating and generating pleasant emotions by paying attention to our focus and actions.

As you review the three equations, notice the one common factor: your sense of personal happiness depends on the choices you make, regardless of your life circumstances.

- **"Equation 1: subjective well-being = genes + circumstance + habits."** The term happiness is too vague and often thought of as laughter and joy. Instead of thinking about happiness, consider your subjective well-being by focusing on questions like, "How would you say you feel today: very happy, pretty happy, or not too happy?" A more detailed self-evaluation option is the Happiness IQ Quick Screen in Appendix B.

- **"Equation 2: habits = faith + family + friends + work."** Long-lasting, subjective well-being is impacted directly by the quality of your social connections. It's beneficial to focus on your social connections with the same discipline as your physical health (e.g., daily exercise). Don't take them for granted; focus on them with intention.

- **"Equation 3: satisfaction = what you have ÷ what you want."** Subjective well-being is learning to become satisfied and content with the life you have. Too many people are caught in mis-wanting ("Once I get X, I'll be happy."). The reality is, what we have now is enough if we can focus and learn to be content.

Case Study: The Pessimist

Kristine is an introvert who regularly tells her few trusted friends that she hates human beings. She's had some terrible experiences in her childhood and was abused in a marriage that ended dramatically. She would describe herself as a pessimistic person who looks for what could be wrong before considering any new opportunity. She's untrusting of others and constantly on guard for them to hurt her. She spends most of her days in a constant state of low energy and unpleasant emotions such as discouragement and pessimism.

She meets a new female friend she likes who happens to be the exact opposite personality. They spend most of their time in pleasant emotions such as gratitude and peace. Kristine enjoys this new person and wants to try to make this new relationship work out. She has enough self-awareness to know that her constant mental state of negativity makes it hard for people to want to be around her.

She asks one of her trusted friends how they became as positive as they are. A psychologist, the friend replies with a smile, "Kristine, we have chatted about this before. You may be surprised at how you will benefit from some training in emotional literacy and practising how to initiate more positive emotions. You have more control over your emotions than you know."

Kristine trusts her friend and is motivated to take some training in emotional literacy. This training provides her with insight into how she can initiate more pleasant emotions by paying attention to where she focuses. Passionate about women in business because she spent years on Wall Street as an executive, she decides to become a mentor. This new passion provides her with many positive things to talk about with her new friend, which fuels engaging and enriching conversations.

Kristine discovers that paying attention to the amount of time she spends each day in unpleasant versus pleasant emotions can help her to hold herself accountable for her emotional well-being. She sets the goal that a good day would be 60 percent pleasant and 40 percent unpleasant. This is a massive improvement, considering she previously lived 80 percent unpleasant and 20 percent pleasant. The lesson for Kristine after months of focus and work is that she has the power from within if she chooses to learn to initiate pleasant emotions on demand by focusing on what she values. She also discovers that there's no need to judge unpleasant emotions, fight them, or allow them to control her mood. Kristine realizes she can influence her mood by what she chooses to focus on.

Some clients tell me they have nothing in their life that's good. This is often because they're only looking at their life through unpleasant emotions. When we still have our breath, things are still okay, as much as we may overlook this gift. When we're feeling emotionally down and overwhelmed, there's no switch that we can flip to change our emotional well-being. Still, we can own what we focus on, which will impact our emotional well-being. Many people get caught in addictions by looking for a quick solution that never makes things better, only worse. The addiction creates a place to hide from accountability, whereas focusing on what we can control opens an opportunity for emotional well-being.

Microskills for Improving Subjective Well-Being

We have a choice when we're aware that we can initiate desirable, pleasant emotions through mindful practice.

Report what worked out well today. A lot of things happen most days that are not all bad for us. To initiate a pleasant mood, focus on what worked out well. Over the next seven-day period, each day, write down three things that went well. Getting to work in your car is an example, because some people didn't get to work safely. Be mindful and open to all that's happening in your life that's going well. Acknowledging the positive can help shift your focus and create pleasant emotions.

Focus on intentional options. Decide where you'll put your energy to influence your emotions. Three options are things you can do alone (e.g., reading to create calm), things you can do with friends (e.g., golfing to have fun), and things you can do that are meaningful (e.g., volunteering to feel you have a purpose). Be mindful of the emotions you want to initiate to positively impact your subjective well-being. This requires you to slow down for a moment to reflect.

Examine how fortunate you are. We all have positive moments, such as graduating from high school. The flip side is, what if you didn't graduate from high school? How could things have turned out differently? Pick one positive event in your life that you value. Starting to realize how fortunate we are can help to initiate pleasant emotions.

Be clear about your strengths. One way to initiate pleasant emotions is to be mindful of your strengths. Pick one each day and notice yourself leveraging this strength. For example, you believe you're a nice person and meet people with positive energy. At the end of the day, reflect on what you did and note how your strength helped others. Notice what pleasant emotions you experience when you do this activity.

Learning how to initiate more positive emotions requires setting realistic expectations. We can learn, provided we're willing to try, to be patient and non-judgemental, and understand that no matter how much work we do, we'll have some days when things don't click as we want. No matter how much we practise and develop our emotional well-being, we're still going to experience unpleasant emotions. How skilled we become at emotional engineering will determine how long before we're experiencing more pleasant emotions.

Happiness Habit

You walk into a meeting room and see a colleague who you've noticed over the years is always smiling and looking happy. This time, she's alone, and you muster the courage to speak to her.

"Hi, how are you? I've seen you here a few times before. If you're okay with it, I'd like to ask a question and learn from you. I can't remember ever seeing you when you weren't smiling. What's your secret?"

Her response: "I focus on what I can control, paying attention to what I'm thinking, and when I do this, I find it easy to feel happy and smile. I spend a lot of time thinking about my family: how grateful I am to have a loving partner and people who care about me. This makes me feel happy."

One way to influence our happiness is to become aware and in tune with our brain when it's not focused on tasks or goals and moves to its default network mode. This mode kicks in like a screensaver that flips on when a computer isn't being used. In this mode, the brain wanders and daydreams. It can tap into positive, negative, or neutral memories that can influence our emotions. Where our mind is focused when we're not fixated on a task or action is important to our mental health and happiness. Learning to master the happiness habit begins with paying attention to the percentage of time our mind focuses on positive versus negative or neutral thoughts. The more we can focus on positive thoughts, the happier we'll be.

REFLECTION

Pick one situation in your life where you would like to experience more pleasant emotions.

- What part of your life: personal, professional, or both?

- What are the top two or three unpleasant emotions you experience most?

- What are you focused on when you're experiencing these emotions?

- What pleasant emotions would you prefer to have?

- What can you do to initiate these pleasant emotions?
  - Leverage your positive emotion generation list.
  - Accept that initiating emotions is not like flipping a switch.
  - Like any skill, it takes time to discover how to label emotions and to learn how to focus on what you want versus what you don't have.

- Now focus your attention on the action you want to engage. Notice how your emotions change as you change your focus.

Think of a time that you would define as being a wonderful and happy moment in your life. Now write about this event and pay attention to the additional details, people involved, and why you enjoyed this moment. When we replay positive memories, we positively influence our emotional state. Building a happiness habit starts with accepting that, although we can't control everything in our life, we can choose what memories we want to focus on. Like any healthy habit, such as exercise and a good diet, training our brain to become happier takes focus and intention. Since we control 40 percent of our happiness, what we focus on plays a significant role in shaping how we perceive our current level of happiness (i.e., emotional well-being), which influences our mood and behaviour.

Focusing daily on building a happiness habit can promote and improve overall mental health and life satisfaction. Happy people typically have higher life satisfaction than less-happy individuals.

Microskills for Facilitating More Pleasant Emotions

Make time each day to notice the good and acknowledge it. Because many of us are moving fast from point A to point B, priority to priority, we may not take time to notice the good things we have. When someone says hello or opens a door for you, offer them a compliment. Take time to stop and see the good in your life.

Change the channel. When your mind starts to wander and you focus on a negative memory, engage in an activity, such as calling a friend, to distract yourself from the negative thinking and memories. The more time we allow our brains to spend wandering through old, unfavourable memories and projecting these as what we can expect in the future, the less likely we'll experience happiness.

Carry positive anchors. Consider putting pictures or short videos on your smartphone that you can use as aids to recall positive memories, like a childhood incident, sporting event, concert, or vacation.

Focus on your strengths daily. Each day, when you're working with others, keep top of mind your two best personal attributes, such as honesty and dependability. Apply these to help you link to your purpose and the kind of person you want to be.

Look forward to interactions. Be open to enjoying all social connections in the workplace by setting positive expectations. When we start with the notion that interactions can be positive, we influence our desire to be open to what can be possible. We can't control how others behave, but we can manage our expectations of what we'd like to see and how we'll behave.

Reserves

Leverage Positive Thoughts to Push Forward

Happiness is not something ready made. It comes from your own actions.

ATTRIBUTED TO THE DALAI LAMA

W HEN YOU look in the mirror, what do you see? What is the first thought that jumps into your head? If you have a positive thought and like what you see, it's because you have decided you like who you are. How you did this is by programming your belief system, which has been influenced by your life experiences such as what others have told you, how you have been treated in the workplace, or, most importantly, what you have told yourself. Assuming you don't have any clinical levels of narcissism and you like what you see when you look at yourself in the mirror, this is an example of how positive thoughts shape how you see the world.

How we see the world is the result of repetition. For example, what we say to ourselves repeatedly is what we will learn to believe is true. Who we are is the net result of what we think over and over. Therefore, there is much advantage to learning how to train our brain to shift its focus, not to run from unpleasant emotions but to ensure they don't pull down our energy levels and prevent us from doing things we enjoy. The term "reserves" in this context refers to building up a belief system that has more positive thoughts than negative. Learning how to create positive thoughts and pleasant emotions on demand will increase the likelihood of having positive emotional well-being that promotes mental health. Reserves help us explore the kinds of knowledge and skills we can use to train our brain to shift its focus to things that are within our control and make good use of our mental energy.

It's much easier to focus *only* on what's not working, what's wrong, or what we don't like. It takes practice and intention to find the positive in challenging moments. It's more helpful to create a mindset that spends more time focusing on positive thoughts than on what's not right or good enough.

How we see the world is influenced by our subconscious, just outside our level of awareness. Many of us are not aware of how the words we say to ourselves or listen to have programmed our belief system. For those living in a state of negativity, this did not happen overnight; it happened because of repetition and because they learned to be negative to protect themselves. When we respond to the world through emotions only, we are not objective. But the brain will do what it is told. We can create a positive belief system.

The Reserves ingredient explores the following:

- How our thoughts affect how we confront unpleasant emotions

- How developing positive thinking can assist in managing unpleasant emotions

- How to create positive thoughts on demand to cope with unpleasant emotions

- Microskills that can be used to facilitate positive thinking

13

Think Good Thoughts

THERE'S WISDOM from every culture, and when we're open to listen, then we are also open to learn. One nugget from Eastern cultures comes from Buddhism, which teaches the value of discovering how to have good thoughts, regardless of our life situation. Why many Buddhists are so peaceful and content is not by chance. It comes out of daily practice that shapes their self-discipline to train their brain that pleasant and unpleasant emotions are nothing more than emotions to notice. The amount of time we spend in pleasant and unpleasant emotions is directly related to what we focus on and think about. This Reserves ingredient offers insights and tips on how to spark more positive thoughts on demand, as well as how to make pleasant emotions where you live most of the time and unpleasant emotions a place you only visit for short periods.

Many of us define happiness by what happens in our life rather than what we think about our current circumstances. Life constantly changes, and nothing is forever. Things we don't want to happen will happen; just because we don't want them to happen doesn't change reality. No matter how upset we get, we can control how we react to our life cir-cumstances. Our thoughts matter as they frame our focus, context, and perceptions.

Rational thoughts can help us make healthy decisions objectively. If you struggle with negative thinking, you can better manage your thoughts through practice. The evidence is abundant: look at the millions of dollars generated by sell-ing cognitive behavioural therapy (CBT) online programs to help people struggling to improve their mental health. The core of CBT is simple: it's about teaching people how to think differently. We don't have to wait until we feel depressed or filled with anxiety to benefit from learning how to think more positively. However, making this change assumes you see value and benefit in learning how to think more positively and promote more emotional well-being.

REFLECTION

Imagine one day your loving partner drops off a card telling you how much they love you. Then within a few hours, you end up in a conversation that makes no sense to you. Your partner becomes overly emotional and, out of a fit of anger, ends the relationship. In those four hours, you go from feeling you're in a loving and secure relationship to being rejected. No matter what emotions or thoughts come up, it doesn't change what just happened. You pause and wait a few days to see if things cool down and try again, with no luck. You're unsure of what happened or why. There was no mature conversation or even an opportunity to work through the conflict.

- Would a situation like this create any negative thoughts for you? Keep in mind that negative thoughts are not the problem; it's what we do with them.

- How do you think you would deal with this situation?

- Life situations like this will happen and you may never understand why. What you do will determine your emotional well-being and predict how long you may experience unpleasant emotions.

Keep in mind that the person who made the decision to break up is a human being trying to do the best they can in that moment to protect themselves. This is why, once we get through our emotions, we should try to pivot and accept that, whatever the reason, some fear (pain) was greater than the reward of the relationship. The *why* really does not matter. Relationships that work are about choice. The goal I would want for a client would be to get them to the point where they accept they are still a good choice for someone, although perhaps not for that person, and to move on to being open to other choices.

Thoughts and emotions are interconnected and fuel each other. Emotions come to the surface faster than conscious thoughts. This is one reason why many without this knowledge act on emotions before thinking out their actions. They haven't been trained not to react to emotions or to debate their thinking before accepting it. Adapting to life's curveballs and challenges and learning how to manage unpleasant emotions better requires training your brain to think positively under pressure. We have the power to train our brain to be kind toward ourselves and others, even in the worst of times.

Your degree of skill in navigating unpleasant emotions and thoughts determines your mindset at any moment. It's okay to feel upset when you experience loss—you can have emotional well-being and be grieving at the same time. This ingredient's focus is what you can do to learn to think more positively so you can build up emotional well-being reserves.

Moving through Curveballs

Life's curveballs can leave us feeling rejected. How we deal with rejection is influenced by our ego strength (i.e., belief in our self-worth to replace the perceived loss) and the perceived value of the loss. The greater the perceived loss, the more likely we'll replay the event, searching for meaning, insight, and reasons. When we begin to replay a life situation in a state of unpleasant emotions, we're at increased risk of looking to place blame on ourselves or others.

During these replays, we may suddenly experience a pang of regret: "If only I would have said..." followed by, "If only I could have, would have, and should have." Regret provides an opportunity to learn from perceived mistakes if we're ready.

The double Rs (rejection and regret) are a challenging combo of unpleasant emotions to take on simultaneously. This combination often happens in relationship breakups. Because intimate social connections are genetically wired, we need them to survive, like food and water. When we suddenly lose a personal social connection, the brain views it like a physical injury and attaches pain. The next unpleasant emotion that joins rejection and regret after a loss is grief. Grief is normal when we experience a personal loss. What's interesting with grief is it facilitates a natural process that triggers different emotions.

Elisabeth Kübler-Ross introduced the five-stage grief model in her book *On Death and Dying* to explain the natural way humans deal with loss (Figure 5). Kübler-Ross developed this model based on her clinical experience working with terminally ill people. Not every person experiencing a loss will go through all five stages. Her point is that the grieving process is not linear; it jumps around based on our thoughts. A person can start their grief process at any stage and move around from stage to stage in any order.[1] Grief is a natural healing process that takes time to move from emotional pain to accepting the loss.

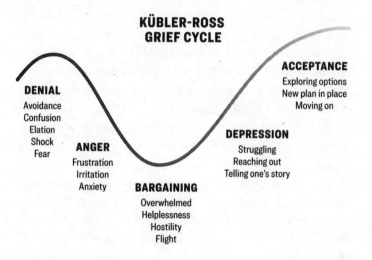

KÜBLER-ROSS GRIEF CYCLE

DENIAL
Avoidance
Confusion
Elation
Shock
Fear

ANGER
Frustration
Irritation
Anxiety

BARGAINING
Overwhelmed
Helplessness
Hostility
Flight

DEPRESSION
Struggling
Reaching out
Telling one's story

ACCEPTANCE
Exploring options
New plan in place
Moving on

FIGURE 5. KÜBLER-ROSS GRIEF MODEL.

The difference between grief and regret is the healing process. Grief has a healing process that's healthy, natural, observable, and expected. Regret doesn't have a natural healing process. Moving past regret is not intuitive; it requires insight, decisions, and commitment to act. Not knowing this is an option explains why we can get trapped in the regret snare. To move out of the regret snare requires both emotional and cognitive regulation.

Cognitive Regulation

Cognitive regulation is our ability to influence the thoughts we have about ourselves and others. The thoughts that run in our head are not by chance; we or others put them there. Our childhood experiences, trauma, current circumstances, and life experiences influence what we believe about ourselves. Fortunately, we can learn to reprogram our brain to think the kinds of thoughts we like to have about ourselves and others. Millions of people don't know that this is remotely possible or that they have any choice over what they think.

Deep in our subconscious mind lie our attitudes and beliefs. We develop attitudes through observation of our environment (e.g., male, and female roles). Beliefs are what we think about ourselves and others that are stored, often outside our awareness. Beliefs can be true or false, as our subconscious mind stores whatever we put into our belief system without prejudice. Learning to manage the belief system is critical for positive mental health and promoting emotional well-being. How well we navigate life's curveballs depends on our attitudes and belief system. Life can be challenging when we fill our belief system with false beliefs (e.g., "I'm dumb."). Negative beliefs are created by accepting flawed logic (e.g., "I can't make any mistakes.").

Exploring how a negative belief system happens:

- You develop beliefs about who you are: "I am…"

- You form core beliefs that influence your conscious and unconscious mind regarding what to think about in a particular situation. In the above example, a person could be confident about who they are in their work life but not their personal life.

- You make decisions based on your current emotions. Emotions are chemicals experienced as feelings attached to a thought and driven by a belief. They're powerful, since they drive behaviour. You're more at risk of making poor decisions when experiencing unpleasant emotions because you feel an urge to get away from them quickly.

- You make decisions about your day-to-day potential based on your belief system built on life experiences. What you choose to do can feel like it makes sense, but if you're not aware of flawed negative beliefs, you become a victim of your belief system, which can negatively impact your emotional well-being.

Shaping a Positive Belief System

How you see and experience the world is much more than just your personality. It starts with what you believe about yourself. For example, do you trust that you're a good person who is loveable, worthy, and good enough?

- **Own your belief system.** Write down all the things you believe about yourself. Only you know the truth. If you're not sure, start journaling and listen to the things you think. For example, suppose you don't ask out a person you're attracted to. Ask yourself why. If you say, "They wouldn't want to go out with me," challenge that thought and ask how you learned that. It's likely because you compare yourself to others and decide whether another person would like you based on looks or status. Emotional change begins with paying attention to your beliefs and challenging them.

- **Stop judging.** Make a conscious effort to stop negative judging of others. Judgement is about being right, about win or lose. It creates internal and sometimes external conflict when we verbalize it. Put your attention into collaboration and focus on the desired outcome and how to get it. Why? Because your subconscious is listening closely to every word. Judgement often comes from a deep worry about what we don't like about ourselves but find in others. The problem is this perception drives our projection and reinforces negative emotion and wiring. We're only hurting ourselves and making our deep, subconscious experience more negative than we want because trained automatic negative thoughts will show up in ways that create discomfort. How many negative thoughts do you think you have a day? The more negative thoughts, the more efficient your brain gets at creating them. It is helpful to keep top of mind that our unconscious mind will do exactly what it is told to believe. This is why there is great value in practising the habit of stopping ourselves from judging self and others.

Researchers at King's College found that constant negative thinking can increase the risk of Alzheimer's disease. A key finding from this study is that negative thinking reduces the brain's ability to think, reason, and form memories.[2] People with high levels of negativity (e.g., constantly cynical) are more at risk of dementia.[3] Donald Hebb is known for saying, "Neurons that fire together wire together," suggesting that the brain is not fixed but is plastic.[4] This means that if being negative has become the way we see the world, we can change how our brain is wired by focusing on positives and stopping our bias for negative thoughts.

Even with the decision to focus more on creating positive thoughts, there will be times when negative thoughts will pop into our head without notice. We'll never be able to get rid of them all. The idea that a negative thought may jump into our head is not the problem; it's what we choose to do once it's there. We can learn how to notice negative thoughts as they occur and not treat them as facts but as random thoughts that have little value to support our emotional well-being. We can use this to initiate and change our focus to switch back to the positive track. The benefit over time is that the focus and practice of wiring our brain to think the way we want it to provides more opportunities to build emotional well-being through improving resiliency, a cognitive skill we can develop. One way to think about resiliency is as the internal belief we can get through a situation based on our resources and support system. Such beliefs fuel our actions to move forward proactively and positively. We can build up our resiliency to have energy stored like a battery we can draw upon in times of need.

Resiliency is not intuitive; it's a trainable skill.[5] When I give talks on building resiliency, I discuss what I call the three *E*s of resiliency: environment (i.e., current circumstances and supports), experience, and education. When it comes to the environment, it's helpful to be aware of our supports, as they're critical for strengthening resiliency. Our personal and professional social connections and our access to support systems (e.g., mental health) influence our confidence in times of need. For example, if you're in an emotional crisis and don't know who to talk to, that can be terrifying compared to having a solid support network and access to professionals.

The decisions we make about the quality of people we associate with also play a role. Hanging around negative people can rub off and make us more prone to negative thinking and accepting flawed assumptions. If we choose positive people who set positive goals for themselves and are kind and caring, we're more likely to find peace and feel supported. As discussed in the Realization ingredient, social contagion can shape mood and thoughts.

Mindful Mindset

What creates space for a mindful mindset is the choice to be mindful. Being mindful is not complex; it involves paying attention to what we're doing and noticing what's happening. This allows us to make decisions and choices about what we want to be thinking versus assuming what comes up in our thoughts by chance. If you'd rather be more positive and create better thinking habits, adopt practices that will accomplish this.

I have adopted Don Miguel Ruiz's Four Agreements:[6]

- "Be impeccable with your word."
- "Don't take anything personally."
- "Don't make assumptions."
- "Always do your best."

This wisdom comes from ancient Toltec standards, a code of conduct that can influence how we interact with the world and increase internal peace, happiness, and the ability to love. What I like about this practice, besides its being hard at times, is how it challenges my belief system as to who I want to be. Deciding to adopt the Four Agreements is not like flipping a switch. It can be a lifetime of work that can help you create the emotional well-being you want.

Mindfulness increases our ability to problem-solve by changing the brain's anterior cingulate cortex and other midbrain regions that participate in emotional regulation and process.[7] Mindfulness helps the brain find calm, enabling us to view the world through a different lens.

We can promote positive and peaceful thoughts by being mindful. It's in this state that we're much more innovative and creative, so that we enjoy each day. As well, we're more ready to deal with the hard days that come. In my view, living a life with no regrets and accepting that we're not perfect but fallible propagates a mindset of hope.

If you wanted to achieve a desired physical goal, such as running ten kilometres, you would need to prepare your body for the task. Sure, some could grind their way through, but many would not be able to keep running for ten kilometres without training and preparation. Training our brain to become more positive creates an opportunity to enjoy each day with the respect and importance it deserves. Not taking each day for granted but living and enjoying it creates a much calmer mind, based on the science of neuroplasticity. This science teaches that the brain is flexible, and if we want to have a calmer and more positive outlook, we need to do things that move us toward being more positive.[8]

Think of one railway track as the negative track and the other as the positive track, so we have two to pick from. When we become aware and intentional, we can train our brain to stop focusing on the negative track and choose the positive one. We can learn to focus on positive thoughts about ourselves and others.

REFLECTION

On a scale of 1 (very easy) to 5 (very hard), rate how difficult it is for you to say the following:

- I'm a good person.
- I'm worthy of love.
- I love myself.
- I trust that I'm good enough as I am now.

How you respond to these will provide you with a window into your belief system. You can have dark corners where you may not fully notice or even be aware of self-doubt and your inner critic. How you tune these down to have less control over you is through intention and committing to accept that it's never the negative thought that's the challenge; it's how much power you give it.

When you choose to put less attention and focus on the negative tracks and put your focus, intention, and energy on learning and practising positive thinking, you're strengthening the positive tracks in your brain that will become the tracks of choice over those old, negative ones.

Introduction to Applied In-vivo Meditation

When you think about meditation, you may view it as something done sitting on a mat or lying down. There are many ways to meditate. The common denominator is they all encourage a quiet space and train the brain to calm down so it's less reactive. In Jon Kabat-Zinn's MasterClass, he points out that we can meditate as much as we want.[9]

The following introduction to in-vivo meditation is based on my personal experience and adaptation of what I learned in Kabat-Zinn's course. Any credit must go to him. When I refer to "in-vivo," it means we can pause at any time and, in the moment, get the benefits of meditation. As well as prevention, meditation can be a way to cope with challenging life moments. We all know there's zero chance we will live our lives without stress. Instead of fighting unpleasant thoughts and emotions with medication, we can create a mental state that reminds us to not judge thoughts. Practising the following steps can help you feel you're in control, rather than being pulled along and reacting to your emotions and negative thoughts that often are not true.

- **Accept the possibility that you have a choice.** For this microskill to work, you must accept that you may have choices when faced with a life stressor, regardless of its intensity. You can learn to become an observer of stress instead of a reactor. As an observer, you don't feel a need to run away from an unpleasant feeling or thoughts that jump into your head, trying to get your attention. This prepares you to notice.

- **Notice.** Life happens fast, and seldom do you get advance notice of unwanted stress. Your body often knows before your brain. For example, you get some bad news, and before you know what's going on, your body's fight-or-flight response has turned on, followed by your conscious brain trying to catch up to understand what has just happened. Simply committing to notice your emotions and not feel you need to react creates space to ground yourself.

- **Ground yourself.** Create more space so you can get your mind and body aligned. Though connected, they don't communicate well with each other under stress. You can't simply say, "Calm down," and your body will understand what to do. However, as Kabat-Zinn teaches, you can always "stop, remember, and drop in." He's referring to what's at the core of all meditation: breath. It's the only constant you can count on at any moment. When you stop thinking about what you're about and remember to focus on your breath, this prepares you to observe.

- **Observe and decide.** You won't stop all your negative thoughts and emotions, but you can learn not to give them so much power. You can accept, observe, and decide where you want to focus. When you put yourself in a position to monitor negative thoughts and unpleasant feelings instead of sitting in them, you're less likely to feel an urge to react. This allows you to consider options to focus your energy so you can cope better with the situation.

It's empowering to learn that we don't need to react to negative thoughts and unpleasant feelings. In-vivo meditation can help us train our brain to be in the moment and focus on the *now*. The more we practise and notice the benefits in our day-to-day life, the more we'll understand the value of mindful practice. It can help create a calm, quiet mind, and we'll discover that we can cope with life stressors and unpleasant emotions.

Consider practising this activity if coping with stress is a struggle. Once you calm your mind, you may be surprised at how small and insignificant things that upset you become.

14

Practise Kindness, Peace of Mind, and Self-Compassion

WE WILL all make mistakes that we will regret. Often it is not the mistake that will define us, however. It is what we think about the mistake. The focus of this chapter is to remind you that what we say to ourselves matters in these challenging moments when faced with an unpleasant emotion or setback.

How much do you think having a good day is due to luck? For some, the quest to have a good day can be akin to finding a four-leaf clover. A common symbol of good luck, a four-leaf clover represents many things, such as hope, wealth, love, and health. However, unless it's given, finding one requires purpose. Good days typically evade us, and when a cycle of bad days becomes a pattern, it's common to think that we're down on our luck.

We may not be able to find a four-leaf clover every day, but we can create goodwill for ourselves and others through kindness. Kindness can be defined as a healthy activity that provides a perceived benefit. Using the four-leaf clover as a framework, we can engage intentional kindness in four areas of life:

- Self-kindness—e.g., enjoy some guilt-free downtime (take thirty minutes to eat lunch quietly).

- Personal life kindness—e.g., help a spouse or family member do a household chore.

- Professional life kindness—e.g., bring one of your teammates a green tea without being asked.

- Public interaction kindness—e.g., slow down and hold a door with a smile for someone and say, "Good morning."

Through self-awareness, we can look for these kinds of opportunities each day.

Our life success and happiness likely involve some degree of luck. For example, showing up at the train station at 8:45 a.m. instead of your usual time of 9:00 a.m. could be the reason you meet a new person who ends up having a profound impact on your career and life. But wishing for such moments can be disappointing. Life happens, and whatever luck we have is by chance and often unplanned. However, we can create our luck by paying attention to what we do each day to help ourselves and others.

Kindness is based on motivation, willingness to suspend judgement, and taking charge of our decisions and actions. Many of us have lists of things we think we need to do daily that make it feel like it's hard to relax or slow down. Intentional kindness is one way to train our brain to be kind to ourselves and enjoy moments in a busy, hectic world. It's not about giving ourselves or others permission to self-medicate to feel better or to avoid responsibilities. It's all about being considerate, concerned, and gentle to ourselves and those around us. If you're tired and struggling to keep up with the demands of the day, allow yourself to say you've had enough and go to sleep. The objective is to feel well-rested and positioned for success to pick up the challenges tomorrow.

To develop your intentional kindness muscle, commit for four weeks to consciously look for at least one opportunity every day to perform an act of kindness in each of the four kindness areas of self, personal, professional, and public. At the end of each day, write out your acts of kindness and score your day on how good it was overall. At the end of the four weeks, compare your scores on the last week to those on the first.

Waiting for good things to happen that can change our life often results in regret. By paying attention to what we do each day, we can improve our experience and create more good days than bad. Being kind to ourselves and others doesn't guarantee that each day will be great, but it reminds us how much our emotional well-being is within our control and that it doesn't take much to help ourselves or someone else feel better.

Random Acts of Kindness

The alarm goes off on Mary's phone, signalling it's time to head out for her 3:00 p.m. appointment. The traffic is heavier than expected, so she's running behind and needs to hurry so she won't be late. She finally gets to the building and sees the elevator door closing as she's running to catch it. Just before the door fully closes, a hand pops out to make the door open again.

Mary jumps on the elevator and, with a smile, thanks the helpful senior citizen. Her response is simple: a smile followed by, "It was my pleasure to help." Mary replies, "Once again, thank you. I find that many of us are often rushing and don't take a moment for a simple act of kindness like you just did for me."

The lady smiles back and says, "I'm sure you'll return the favour to someone else, as it doesn't take much effort to be kind."

Performing an act of kindness shifts our attention to a positive thought, which can be helpful when our mind is busy worrying or stressing. Keeping up with all the demands of life can feel like a grind. The kind lady who held the door for Mary demonstrated how little effort it can take to help another person meet a need. Acts of kindness begin with a level of awareness outside of ourselves and a willingness to help another person or provide a spontaneous gift. Helpfulness benefits the receiver and giver when done with no expectation of receiving anything in return.

Be open to the notion that doing something nice for another person—regardless of how small the act of kindness—can benefit both parties. Many of us have days when we're on a treadmill that has us constantly rushing from point A to point B to keep up with the day's demands. This drive to keep up can result in tunnel vision, and we neglect to pay attention to what's around us. Acts of kindness are often spontaneous. It doesn't take planning or a lot of effort to participate, only a willingness to notice and be open to opportunities to be kind to a stranger or someone we know. Luckily, there are many kind people, and acts of kindness happen every day. We'll all be healthier and happier if we can experience and perform acts of kindness for others.

Microskills for Becoming More Engaged with and Aware of Kindness

Opt into kindness. Benefitting from acts of kindness requires accepting their benefits. One way to explore the benefits is to perform three simple acts of kindness over the next twenty-four hours. For example, hold the door open for a colleague or put extra water in the kettle at work to be ready for the next person.

Define what random acts of kindness mean to you. Acts of kindness are things we do for people we know or don't know to help them meet a need. Acts of kindness can range from opening a door to doing something for another person with the intention to help them or to just make their day. It's helpful to brainstorm the many opportunities you have each day to do things for others without being asked, such as giving compliments, giving gifts, saying kind words, showing gratitude, and doing an act of service for someone.

Promote social kindness. Commit to not engaging in any gossip or complaining about others behind their backs. People can be cruel to each other. When we commit to not teasing or judging others, we help stop and prevent peer negativity.

Notice the benefits. Notice how you feel when you perform an act of kindness. If you feel regret or any other negative emotion, it isn't an act of kindness. Noticing how you feel reinforces the benefits and strengthens the likelihood you'll do more things for others.

Peace of Mind

Peace of mind is when we're calm and content. We have no regrets or concerns; we're just fine. Simple actions such as going for a walk that uncovers a breathtaking view, creating a moment of pause and a sense of calm and peace, can influence peace of mind. At such a moment, the world stops, and life is pure.

In the age of the 24/7 media cycle dominated by the world's economic and political uncertainty, many people's minds are cluttered and filled with stress and anxiety. Too many are living on autopilot; days and weeks fly by. Some are caught on a treadmill, trying to get through each day and keep up with the grind. Moments of internal peace and calm can be elusive.

Peace of mind begins with paying attention to conversations we have with ourselves at home and work. Life moves fast, so when we can stop and enjoy what we have, we're better able to experience peace of mind. Mental health is shaped by what we think and do daily. Actively seeking peace of mind is one proactive way to affect our mental health positively.

Microskills for Promoting Peace of Mind

Some of us under stress look for peace of mind in the wrong way, such as through alcohol or gambling. But there are healthy alternatives that require only intention and daily focus.

Nurture your peace of mind. Nurturing peace of mind through mindful, small actions can fuel hope, a feeling that influences the belief that things will be okay. Take two minutes out of your day to find quiet at home and work to calm and refocus your thoughts.

Find a mental anchor. Envisage a magical sunset or memory of when you were inspired, awed, and at peace. What were you doing, how did you feel, and how did you know it was an incredible experience? These memories and feelings are anchors. The goal is to open your mind to previous experiences or the possibility of how these moments resulted in brief periods of pure peace.

Take an inventory. Make a list of things you can do today that can nurture peace of mind. Some people practise daily meditation. For others, a nature walk is an excellent gateway. Pick one thing you do or are willing to learn or start that will open the door to moments that nurture peace of mind. There are many options; your mind just needs to be open. Each day offers a sunrise and a sunset. They're free, and they bring moments of peace for many.

Make a commitment. Achieving peace of mind requires intention, planning, and follow-through. One universal truth for every human being is the desire for peace. Life is short, and we can't change the past. What we can do is live for today. In a world with lots of noise, stimuli, and information, committing to finding moments of peace can help us feel contentment and reduce our stress at home and work.

Self-Compassion

It's normal when you awake each morning to start to think about what you have coming up in the day ahead regarding your family, personal life, or work. For some, this process can fire off thoughts and emotional pangs of anxiety about what lies ahead. The causes of these pangs of anxiety may be fears about failing at work or not being good enough in some aspect of your job, such as meeting with a manager or making a presentation. The root cause of some of this fear may be the conscious or unconscious drive for perfection. A perfectionist sets high standards that leave little room for thinking about failure and no room for experiencing failure.

Accepting that perfectionism is an unrealistic goal is one of the first steps to reducing anxiety. There's little probability that any human being will not make mistakes. No one can be perfect all the time, regardless of their dedication, intentions, desire, or skill set. Instead, replace the desire to be perfect with a commitment to excellence. Achieving excellence is committing to being the best you can by taking the best actions you can. Reframing your view can help you understand that all you can do is try to do your best. Once you realize that it's unrealistic to expect to be perfect all the time, you position yourself to accept that as hard you try, you may not always be successful.

One way to deal with failure is to learn and practise self-compassion. Self-compassion is like supporting someone you care about through a difficult time. It begins with acknowledging that when you fail, it's difficult, but it's important to not ignore or accept the failure. Like any skill, self-compassion takes practice if we're going to be able to comfort ourselves and turn off self-attacks, shame, and criticism. Self-compassion can help us face challenges such as dealing with regret or other unpleasant emotions when we judge ourselves negatively.

Eastern thinking offers the idea that our automatic, negative thoughts are nothing more than thoughts. Accepting this can facilitate self-compassion. Our thoughts are just random information with no evidence that they're true. When you don't hyper-focus on negative thoughts that lead to negative feelings, you create an environment in which they'll leave as fast as they come.

REFLECTION

- While you can't try to do everything at once, you may notice you could benefit from all of the above. Pick one microskill from this chapter you'll consider practising for the next ninety days. It typically takes a few months for a new practice to start to feel comfortable, genuine, and meaningful. We need time to turn down the inner critic who will not go away quietly. Positive change requires time, patience, and empathy.

- Ask yourself, "When was the last time I felt peace of mind?" What were you doing when you had this feeling?

15

Preparing Your
Mind to Be Positive

NOW IT'S time to remove assumptions and be direct with yourself. Do you want to be a positive person: yes or no? Though the response seems obvious, remaining negative is easier than taking ownership of your thinking and doing the hard work to change how you view the world. Change is hard, and there's nothing wrong with recognizing this fact. But we can learn to have better emotional well-being if we're willing to do the work, one key piece of which is taking charge of our thinking and refusing to allow flawed beliefs to rule us.

How you prepare you mindset with intention will influence how you cope with any unpleasant emotion, particularly regret. The expression "the best defence is a good offence" in this context refers to the fact that training your brain to be positive will give you the capacity to better manage challenging moments. What matters is not what happens but how we cope with it. I believe this is a critical ingredient for not getting stuck in regret.

The Power of Positive Self-Talk

What do you say to yourself when you look in the mirror first thing in the morning? Whether your response is positive or negative, the science of self-talk suggests that your inner voice's opinions and evaluation will have a significant impact on how you think about yourself.[1] This will directly impact your confidence in personal and professional situations.

The goal of positive self-talk is to increase the positive conversations you have with yourself to improve your mental health at work and home. Self-talk can be destructive or constructive. Individuals with destructive self-talk are critical of themselves: e.g., "I'm a failure; I should have figured out how to get the agreement done." This type of constant, negative self-talk that devalues your self-worth can negatively impact your mental health.

Constructive self-talk focuses on facts and looks for the positive: e.g., "We didn't come to an agreement this time, but I'm pleased I held my position. There will be another opportunity." Self-talk research suggests that the more you put yourself down, second guess yourself, and view change as negative, the less likely you'll be able to cope with and solve problems under pressure.[2] This research also suggests that individuals with active, destructive self-talk are more likely to quit and have more stress than those who practise positive self-talk.

One consequence of destructive self-talk is confirmation bias.[3] In the above example, if no one challenges the person's assessment that they're a failure, it confirms their hypothesis that they won't find an agreement and there's no sense trying again.

If your self-talk mercilessly judges you negatively, this is not helpful for your overall mental health. Only you can decide if you want to influence your positive self-talk. Learning how to turn off negative self-talk and replace it with positive statements doesn't happen overnight. It takes focus, persistence, and patience. The good news is that it can become a habit that can positively impact your mental health.

Shaping self-talk starts with understanding the kinds of internal conversations you have on a typical day. Getting a baseline requires keeping a score of your self-talk. Each time you say something positive to yourself, give yourself a point. For each negative thought you find yourself having in a day, take away one point. At the end of the day, your score will be either positive or negative. Get your average over three days.

Microskills for Promoting Positive Self-Talk

Catch and release. When you catch yourself saying something negative (e.g., "I'm stupid; I should have known she wouldn't ask me to be a part of the project."), challenge it ("What are my facts that she doesn't like me? Why else could I not have been picked for the team?"). Once you challenge the thought, you're ready to release the destructive self-talk and replace it with constructive statements. You can create the story you want: "I'd like to have been picked; however, I'm sure she has her reasons. I'll keep working hard, she'll notice, and maybe I'll be offered the next project."

Smell the roses. Life moves fast. When you notice something simple that you enjoy, practise acknowledging with your internal self-talk what's positive, why, and how fortunate you are to have the moment. Whether what you notice is perfect is not the point; find the good and enjoy it for a moment. Look for one of these moments each day. It's okay to permit yourself to smile outside and inside during these moments.

Anchor positive self-talk. Recall positive personal experiences that inspire you. Positives are all around us; we need to notice them: from the clean air we breathe and water we drink to our family and friends. When you have time, such as while commuting, pick and play a positive story or event that makes you feel good and proud of yourself. Focus on this moment as long as you can. The more you do this, the more anchored this story will become in your mind.

Talking about being positive and becoming positive are two different realities. There's no positive pill. While some of us make more serotonin and oxytocin than others and may naturally have more biology working in our favour, we all have choices, regardless of our genetic destiny. Training our brain to become positive requires self-discipline and practise until it becomes a habit.

REFLECTION

How you respond to the following six points can give you a sense of where you are on the positive-thinking continuum.

- What are your top three most valuable personal strengths, and why do you believe so?

- Do you accept that you don't have to be perfect and that making mistakes is a part of being human? It's difficult to learn to live life with no regrets if you can't accept this fact.

- Do you accept that asking for support and getting help is not a sign of weakness when you're stressed?

- Do you set your intention for what you want to accomplish each day to ensure you're not living on autopilot?

- Do you accept that you can learn how to have more positive thoughts every day?

- Do you understand that there are no shortcuts and that the path to developing a positive mental outlook is practice?

Benefits of Developing Delayed Gratification

Immediate gratification is a modern-day problem. Studies have tested this by offering a person $50 now or $100 in one year.[4] A person driven by immediate gratification takes the $50, but the patient person is able to wait for more money. The research explains that the ventral striatum part of the brain plays a role in why some have developed an impulse for immediate gratification. A patient person has increased activity in the anterior prefrontal cortex that prompts them to shift their focus to imagining what it would be like to get this reward in the future. Seeking immediate gratification can put you at risk of making kneejerk decisions focused on feeling good that can negatively impact your future. Developing emotional well-being means resisting the urge for the quick, feel-good options life offers and learning to sit with unpleasant emotions as we practise and discover new habits that can have a long-term benefit.

The famous marshmallow experiment provides an applied example of delayed gratification.[5] In this experiment, the researcher left a room for fifteen minutes, leaving children with two options: 1) they could eat the marshmallow or 2) they could wait until the researcher got back and be rewarded with a second marshmallow. The findings from this study revealed that children who waited for the second marshmallow were much less likely to engage in at-risk behaviour as adults. They had higher SAT scores and reported a more fulfilling life—all because they were able to think about the long-term gains and resist the urge for immediate gratification.

As suggested a few times in this book, developing emotional well-being requires patience—the ability to stay calm while waiting for an outcome that we need or want.[6] It's a critical skill but can be hard to learn. Recognizing that everything we want will not happen immediately helps us create a more stable and realistic mindset. Accept that change is a process, and if it were easy, there would be much less stress and frustration in the world. Technology, for all its positive elements, has resulted in a mindset of quick and fast gratification. Being impatient and in a rush doesn't just affect our current emotional state, however. It can also influence how others see us—it seldom is viewed by others as a desirable attribute. Learning to become more patient requires intention and self-discipline.

Microskills for Improving Your Patience Factor

Set expectations. Decide that you want to be more patient. Acknowledge how being impatient has created stress in your life. Sit in these thoughts for a moment. Remember how people reacted to you at such a time. Now think of a time you observed someone being patient and how people responded to them. It's helpful to reinforce in your mind why being patient is valuable and decide that you want to be patient.

Practise empathy. Learning to be more patient is a process and requires rewiring and training your brain. Suspend judgement and practise empathy, meaning you're clear on what you want, and when you fail, you won't judge yourself; you'll look for what you can learn.

Define triggers. We typically have a trigger that frustrates our patience, whether a child, partner, peer, pet, or desired outcome. One researcher suggested triggers come in three main varieties: interpersonal patience, life hardship patience, and daily hassles patience.[7] These are preloaded and can automatically fire off impatient behaviours such as irritability, frustration, and judgement. Write out your triggers, then pick your top two and decide that you will create more space with these. Focus on being calm and respectful of others and accept that you can't get everything when you want it. Sometimes, slowing down for two minutes and just breathing can be enough. This is about mindset and expectations.

Journal your experience. At the end of each of the next ninety days, reflect on when you were patient and when you were not. This will ensure you're aware and help you recommit to this desired outcome. The goal is to make your next-day plan before you go to bed each night.

Practise Optimism

Optimism is about openness to the possibility that things will be okay or can be better. It helps to calm the mind from worry. You can get your optimism baseline by going to Appendix C and completing the Optimism Quick Screen. It can be helpful to repeat this measure every month to monitor how your practice is working.

The degree of time you naturally engage in optimistic versus pessimistic thinking shapes your emotional well-being when you experience pleasant and unpleasant emotions. A pessimistic person spends more time in unpleasant emotions as they're more fearful that things will go wrong for them. If you're overly pessimistic, you'll be quicker to conclude that something can't be done during a stressful period and tend to focus on what's wrong. In this state, it's common to immediately take a negative view and utter disempowering statements that create negative beliefs and serve no long-term benefit, such as, "I should have expected I wouldn't get this right." When we're more pessimistic than optimistic, we tend to be more critical, judgemental, and negative.

The following statistics point out why optimism matters in life and work:[8]

- 75 percent of optimists received a positive performance rating at their last job evaluation, compared to 24 percent of pessimists.

- 84 percent of optimists thrive in high-pressure situations and cope well with stress, compared to 24 percent of pessimists.

- Optimism is a better predictor of employee engagement than pessimism.

REFLECTION

- Spend a moment enjoying positive experiences to train your brain that good things matter. Moving from the hyper-reactive brain that's amazing at finding what's wrong with the world requires transferring energy to shaping a new, positive lens. Accepting that there may be a delay in moving from feeling you're living life with more negative than positive thoughts is a journey, and there will be a temptation to look for a quick fix or to give up.

- Generating more positive thinking requires a decision. It doesn't need to be overly complicated. Just ask yourself, "Do I want more positive thinking in my life?" If yes, pick a microskill and allow your brain to create new wiring. All you need to do is practise.

Research at Harvard suggests that highly motivated and positive leaders who believe in their ability and their team's ability to achieve their goals shape the future.[9] There are benefits for leaders to own their behaviour and understand how their behaviour and words can shape and inspire their employees to follow them. Those who take an optimistic outlook each day are confident, positive, and focused on achieving a goal. They know there will be bumps and hard work, and they're not over-confident. They're centred, believe in focusing on what they can control, and see value in being positive and hopeful. They want to provide their employees with the certainty that their leader will remain calm and confident and that together the team can succeed.

It's hard to change brain wiring, but it takes no more energy to train it to be positive than negative. Be intentional, and when a negative thought jumps in, train your brain with the following: "This option is not my preference. What is a possible positive, alternative thought?" This process will get easier through intention and repetition once your brain learns that you prefer positive alternatives that are hopeful.

Microskills for Developing Optimism

Take the thirty-day challenge. For the next thirty days, set a rule that you're not allowed to say out loud anything negative about yourself, anyone else, or any situation. When asked your opinion, you can say, "I'm not sure, but I'm hopeful for some positive outcome."

Define what optimism means to you. Take a moment and visualize how an optimistic versus pessimistic person would behave in your role. If you're unclear, do a bit of research and reading on the value of optimism and why and how it is important for our emotional well-being (such as listening to Simon Sinek's podcast *A Bit of Optimism*, particularly the episode "The One with Brené Brown."[10]). Become clear on how your words and energy affect others for good and bad.

Focus on what's right first. For instance, an optimistic leader can be tough and direct and challenge their employees' work. However, they do best by committing to focusing on what's right first and why it's important before exploring what's wrong and needs to be improved. This can give employees the fuel and inspiration to feel good about what they've done and take ownership before they go back and make recommended changes.

It's okay to smile. By being aware and open to smiling when interacting with others, you're projecting optimism through your non-verbal communication. This practice can positively impact your mental state, and a positive mental state has you better prepared for the challenges that require your calm, optimistic, and steady hand. Some say it takes only seventeen muscles to smile and forty-three to frown, so save some energy.

Practise developing your coping skills to solve problems. Perhaps one of the best skills for developing optimism is having confidence in your ability to solve problems. If this is a gap, you can develop these skills through training, coaching, and mentoring. The more confident you are in your ability to solve problems, the easier it is to believe that you'll find a tolerable solution.

16

Wiring a
Positive Mindset

THE PATH to a positive mindset runs through practice. When faced with challenging life moments when you're trying to move past regret, how well you've learned to manage your unpleasant emotions and negative thinking is the foundation that will support change.

As noted, there are no shortcuts or magic pills for creating a more positive mindset. You must be intentional and committed to training your brain to wire and fire new, positive thoughts and emotions that lay positive tracks. The challenge with habits is that they can take time to build—and much less time to break. Researcher Phillippa Lally found that it can take a person 18 to 254 days to create a new habit, with the average being 66 days.[1] James Clear, the author of *Atomic Habits*, offers the practical wisdom that one key to maintaining habits is not breaking the chain. He means that if you miss a day, get back to practising the habit as quickly as possible. Just thinking about the habit you're forming, even if you're not giving it 100 percent, is better than not doing anything.[2]

The "Thirty-Day Negative Thought Stop" Challenge

There's no substitute for action. Changing means doing something. So, plan to accept and start the "thirty-day negative thought stop" challenge. If successful, you'll notice improvement within the month. This experience can help you discover how your intentional actions can shape your mood and emotional well-being. Reducing negative thinking is not as complex as some may believe; it often requires just deciding to do it. However, some who have clinical issues may need support to learn how to cope with anxiety and depression.

This thirty-day challenge can help bring to your level of awareness what you believe you want to do and think can happen. Being more positive begins with intention and belief. Here's how to launch into your challenge:

- **Get a negative thoughts baseline.** On the first day, every time you have a negative thought, record it. Don't judge the thought or the number of thoughts you have. Notice how many times you have a negative thought about yourself or another person. You may miss a few, since the brain is fast. Don't fret about it; just get a baseline number.

- **Be honest with yourself.** Track your negative thoughts every day for the next twenty-nine days and set a goal of improving a bit each day.

- **Don't expect perfection.** The goal is to average fewer negative thoughts each day by the final week.

- **Begin your challenge consciously.** Set the expectation with your powerful conscious brain to be more positive. This means committing to not complaining or joining in on any negative group thinking. This one decision can help create more of a pause so you avoid engaging in negative thinking. Listen to yourself carefully. You may be surprised at how this can help you edit and reduce the number of negative thoughts you share with others.

- **Notice negative thoughts as they come into your head.** As a negative thought comes to mind, treat it with curiosity. Ask, "Why am I having this thought now?" Look for the *why*, and you may find it's linked to an expectation or a belief. It's these little acts that can start to rewire your brain. Instead of negative thoughts showing up when they want, they become passing thoughts you don't fully buy into.

- **Trade in negative thoughts for positive ones.** The mind is quite interesting. If you have a negative thought (e.g., "I'm dumb; I can't believe I made this mistake."), you can train your brain so that when you notice a negative thought, you trade it for a positive one. Instead of focusing on and replaying "dumb," think of when you last felt confident and competent and how much time and learning it took to get to that point. By sitting in this replay of positive thinking for about twenty seconds, the brain discovers that success is a process, and there are often potholes along the way.

- **Evaluate your day and set expectations for tomorrow.** At the end of each day, self-evaluate your level of commitment and attention to your thirty-day challenge. Without any judgement, review where you could improve and set that as your expectation for tomorrow. The thirty-day challenge is not about perfection; it's about making small changes and accepting that you have more control over your thinking than you may have believed.

Practise Gratitude Daily with Intention

What are you most grateful for? When we're in unpleasant emotions and feeling stuck, we're more prone to thinking everything is terrible, since we're seeing the world through a moment in time. It's not a fair representation of all we have in this world; it's merely a distortion.

Research suggests a link between the benefits of gratitude—the practice of counting your good fortune, such as having health, feeling safe, and having a loving family and friends—and your well-being.[3] Your emotional well-being is influenced by what you focus on daily. If you focus on the positive, you'll likely feel more positive. I've named this the 98–2 theory.[4] It's common for a person to report that 98 percent of their day is going well and 2 percent is not. Frequently, however, 98 percent of their focus is on the 2 percent that's not going so well. This can cloud their perceptions and instill a negative bias regarding how well their life is going. It can also affect their level of stress and sense of balance and calm.

Whether or not you perceive that your day is going well, you can probably still find things to be grateful for if you look. So, what are you grateful for? Have you thought about that recently? For some people, learning to be grateful takes practice, but it's not hard to take a moment a few times each day to reflect and acknowledge what you must be grateful for. You can do this consciously or in writing. I like to call it "an attitude of gratitude." The benefits of having an attitude of gratitude are wide-ranging, such as improving your relationships, physical health, psychological health, sleep, self-esteem, and mental health.[5]

This daily practice can quickly shift your focus from complaining about what you don't have or think you deserve to what's positive and beneficial. Gratitude comes in many forms. Expecting your car to start on a minus-35-degree Celsius Canadian winter night may seem trivial until the battery can't crank the engine. It's helpful to learn how not to allow expectations to blind us from being grateful for the little and big things that are working well.

Gratitude research suggests that practising gratitude can help you deal with adversity, create positive emotions and energy, and enjoy life better.[6] Research sources endorse the value of adding a daily dose of gratitude to promote overall health.[7] It costs nothing to acknowledge yourself or others each day. When done authentically, it makes you feel good. It can fuel life satisfaction and contentment and become a positive boost. When practised regularly, it can provide a positive reserve to draw upon when you feel stressed and challenged.

Microskills for Daily Gratitude Practice

Acknowledge at least *one* positive action, person, or thing that will charge your gratitude battery. Look for it in the quiet moments, like when you first wake up or at the end of your day. There's something to be grateful for every day if you give yourself a chance to look. Whenever you're focused on something positive, you're giving your mind a break from negativity, and that can improve your mood and outlook.

Take time each day to focus on what you're grateful for. It is a discipline that takes practice for long-term mental health. Remind yourself that being alive is something to be grateful for.

Creating Fun Is Good for Emotional Well-Being

Why are many children so happy? Because they play and have fun as much as possible. Some of us have lost this priority as adults and replaced it with others. Making time for fun is a simple and potent medicine for emotional well-being.

The word "fun" means enjoyment, amusement, and entertainment. How people have fun varies from unplanned moments that happen because they're open to pausing and enjoying them, such as a funny email or a funny story from a peer, to planned moments of meeting friends or engaging in personal passions.

How much fun do you have each day? Do you intentionally plan for it? People have different definitions of fun, different perceptions of their ability to have fun, and different reasons they can or can't have fun. Consider how each of the following people may answer the question of how much fun they have each day:

- A person hyper-focused on their career and committed to getting ahead

- A person experiencing a mental health issue and struggling emotionally

- A person in a job they don't enjoy

- A person happy with their career

- A person overwhelmed by the demands of home and work

- A person in a caretaking role after work hours

- A person experiencing a chronic health issue

Some will find this challenge harder than others. The ways we can have fun are unlimited because the possibilities are endless.

Fun Mnemonic

Certain factors contribute to our ability to have fun:

- **F**—Free from tension, pressure, and responsibilities
- **U**—United and connected with the present (being in the now)
- **N**—Nice to yourself and others, generating positive emotions and feelings

Life is busy for most people, whether we're working in or outside the home. Fun can feel elusive or like something we'll get to when there's time. Ask yourself: "On a scale of 1 to 10, how satisfied am I with the amount of fun I have daily?" Any score less than 5 suggests that you could benefit from more fun. If your score is 9 or 10, it may be worth asking yourself if the amount of fun you're having is putting any responsibilities or relationships at risk.

Finding a healthy balance of fun is one element of a fulfilling life. The average person won't get to the point where 100 percent of their day-to-day existence is fun. While there are such people, when it comes to fun, most find a healthy balance between fun and everyday responsibilities. The first step is to take an honest look at the amount of fun you're having and whether you want to add more to your life. Or perhaps you're considering having a bit less fun and shifting this time to achieving a goal that you may have been putting off.

Some people simply don't make having fun a priority. They're more focused on the tasks they believe they need to do to be responsible and achieve their goals. Others may be having too much fun and allowing some of their responsibilities to slip. Taking charge of the amount of fun we have begins with putting things in context regarding our daily reality and challenges. This can help determine the path we take to manage our fun. There's nothing wrong with aspiring to have more fun if it doesn't negatively impact our commitments, health, safety, or others around us. Healthy fun is good for mental health and happiness.

Any activity that we enjoy doing that brings joy and laughter creates the pleasant emotion we know as "fun." Even when we're unable to go out and socialize, we can find fun in many ways. For me, one way to have fun whenever I want is to play fetch with my bulldog, Link. He is always ready to go, and my heavens, the joy I get from him brings a level of fun to my life I would not have it were not for him! I also enjoy my Sunday night calls with my brothers, my Monday noon call with my friend Richie, and texting my friends to check in—they'll often send something funny that will get me laughing. Remember, fun does not need to be complicated! What we can benefit from is being aware of what we find fun and ensuring we create space for it. Make creating pleasant emotions and fun a priority.

REFLECTION

Explore the degree of fun you'd like to have. Will you decide you want to have a little healthy fun daily? We each have a different set of preferences for what fun is and how we have it. It may be watching a funny TV show, calling a friend, going to lunch, playing a round of golf, or walking a pet.

- Define what fun is for you.

- Write out at least three ways you believe you can have fun. Be specific on why each planned or unexpected way is fun for you. Like any activity in life, having fun requires knowing what defines it and making it a priority.

- Schedule your fun activities weekly, at a minimum. Highlight how you'll have fun and with whom.

- It doesn't need to be a formal plan, but a busy life can get filled with pressing priorities if you don't protect time for fun.

- To have planned fun, you must make fun time important.

- If you want to have more or less fun but you're unsure where to start, this can be the first step to engaging in conversations with trusted peers or a mental health professional about the topic.

Reset

How to Get Back on Track

Happiness is not a goal,
it is a by-product.

ELEANOR ROOSEVELT

LIFE CAN take us on road trips (and sometimes detours) that we may or may not want. Detours can cause us to make kneejerk decisions that result in regret. Living in regret or any other unpleasant emotion can be painful and challenging. When we're stuck in an unpleasant emotion, it is normal to want to escape pain. Therefore, many people engage in at-risk behaviours that result in poor lifestyle choices or habits that can have a negative impact on their physical and emotional well-being. The Reset ingredient is like an emotional first-aid kit. The sole purpose is to take accountability for behaviours that are not in our long-term best interest. Mind tricks can fool us into believing that engaging in five hours of video games every night, for example, is the only or best way to create pleasant emotions, and they can blind us to the impact these feel-good behaviours may have on others or ourselves. Only you will know if there are things you are doing to cope with unpleasant emotions that you know are most likely not in your best interest.

How can we hit "reset" when falling into problem behaviours? One of our biggest challenges is dealing with unpleasant emotions. The number of people addicted to drugs, alcohol, sex, gambling, the Internet, and videos is not by chance. Without insight and lacking knowledge and skills, too many are motivated to get away from emotional pain as fast as possible. The path to escape unpleasant emotions is often impulsive, reactive, and short-sighted.

When we ignore the consequences of at-risk behaviours because we believe we need to feel better, we increase our risk of engaging in behaviours that put us on track for an addictive disorder such as substance use or gambling. I have completed a post doc in addictive disorders at UCLA School of Medicine, written books on the topic, and worked for many years in addictive disorders, and I have concluded that most of these addictive disorders develop because of an inability to tolerate unpleasant emotions and move away from them in a healthy way. The cure for unpleasant emotions is learning how to live with them.

The Reset ingredient is not therapy, nor is it treatment. You use it when you need to move away from at-risk behaviours, such as moderate to heavy alcohol use, before they become habits or addictions. If you have a problem with any type of substance use or behaviour, talk with your doctor or mental health professional about options to get the support you need. The Reset ingredient falls under the umbrella of prevention and can reduce the negative hold unpleasant emotions have on thinking and behaviours.

This ingredient includes the following key points:

- A path out of a regret loop of engaging in coping behaviours

- How at-risk behaviours can result in poor coping skills that mask unpleasant emotions and can lead to more serious issues such as addiction

- A strategy to break out of at-risk behaviours before they become habits or addictive disorders

Tackling Stress and Self-Deception

M OST HAVE heard the old expression that you can be guaranteed two things: death and taxes. There's a third. You can be sure you're going to experience unwanted, negative stresses and unpleasant emotions. Some will originate from decisions and thoughts; others will come from external sources such as work and family (and death and taxes). No matter the source, we have no choice other than to behave.

Any type of stress can trigger the biological response understood as the general adaptation syndrome.[1] In this state, the brain is hyper-alert, the heart rate increases, breathing quickens, adrenaline is released, and the digestive and immune systems shut down because they're nonessential in a crisis. This state is also known as fight or flight, where the sympathetic nervous system takes over the body to protect it. Not until the stress is perceived to be gone does the parasympathetic nervous system return the body to homeostasis.[2]

Unwanted (bad) stress is anything creating concern, fear, or worry. As we move through life, we experience degrees of unwanted stress that can be defined as small or big potholes, minor or major setbacks, or unforeseen events like divorce, death, injury, and illness that change our trajectory.

As challenging as it can be for some, it's not the frequency, intensity, or duration of unwanted stress that determines reputation and emotional well-being; it's what we do when we're experiencing it. Our actions sometimes can make our situation move from emotionally challenging to emotionally complex. How effectively or ineffectively we cope with bad stress influences our emotional well-being. By remaining calm and not reacting emotionally in stressful situations, we can tolerate stress so that it doesn't control our emotions. Several things, including genetics, social supports, financial health, lifestyle habits, and coping strategies, can impact stress tolerance.

If you watch a Navy SEALs YouTube training video, you'll see that the training teaches stress tolerance. Training is focused on learning not only how to fight their enemy but also how to fight their mind. Many SEALs will tell you that a significant insight is discovering that their mind will want to quit before their body. Through painful, stressful experiences, successful SEALs can tame their minds of fear, allowing them to tolerate intense stress while staying composed and focused on their mission. They're not having a super time when experiencing physical pain, but they've learned through their training that it's mandatory to stay calm, think clearly, and focus on their desired outcome.

Learning to cope with unwanted stress requires learning how to manage unpleasant emotions effectively. The chapters on realization, reputation, and reserves provide insights into coping better with unpleasant emotions. Not knowing or accepting that we have free will is why many people are overwhelmed by unpleasant emotions and negative thoughts.

Being in constant emotional pain triggers the subconscious mind to look for options to stop or dull the pain to feel better.

How Mind Tricks Can Sneak Up On Us

Mind tricks influence flawed thinking and behaviours to cope with unpleasant emotions like regret. They convince us to accept a line of thinking and that the behaviours offered are the best choices to tame unpleasant emotions. Mind tricks are deceptive, as they put our focus on a feel-good behaviour and have us dismiss any concerns about the risk to our health. They can leave you feeling powerless, explaining why sometimes a person may get stuck in regret or another unpleasant emotion not for days but years.

A mind trick is about creating a desired state that will influence our perceptions of a situation, such as being stressed out about work and worried about our future. Engaging in alcohol consumption can be a choice to change one's emotional state to numb or distract emotional pain. One downside of chronic alcohol consumption is that, as a depressant, it can lead to a substance-use dependency that increases the risk of depression. Consumption of alcohol starts as an escape that can become a mental prison for those who get trapped in the mind trick, believing there's no choice but to keep drinking, which ends in a substance-use dependency. Perhaps one of the most challenging concerns is food addiction (e.g., eating when not hungry) to escape emotional pain, increasing the risk of excessive daily calorie intake affecting diabetes, obesity, and cardiovascular disease.

Through thirty-plus years of publishing, researching, and working in the field of addictive disorders, I've never met someone who could honestly say that engaging in substance-use dependency is good for them or their future. However, this knowledge alone is not always enough for them to find the motivation to stop. Stopping any behaviour begins with a desire. No one can make another person change their behaviour. Focusing on what we want and being clear on why leads to change. Once we get this, we're on track to begin the journey and achieve desired outcomes.

Most at-risk behaviours (also known as maladaptive coping skills) create the illusion of short-term symptom relief from unpleasant emotions. They come in many forms: food, the Internet, social media, drugs, alcohol, shopping, sex, work, and gambling. Doing any of these behaviours once is not a problem, in most cases, unless they involve highly dangerous and addictive drugs or potent opioids. Drinking a bottle of wine with your partner on Friday night is not an at-risk behaviour. However, drinking two bottles every night by yourself in a relatively short time can put you on track for moving from substance abuse to substance-use dependency.

Why We Deceive Ourselves

Many get caught up in mind tricks and engage in at-risk behaviours because of a lack of knowledge and skills to cope. Self-deception, the mental process of denying or rationalizing decisions, can blind us to the fact that what we're doing is harmful. We can use self-deception to convince ourselves that our thinking makes more sense than some counter-position for our current circumstances.

Self-deception can be a double-edged sword. It can limit you from believing in your potential (e.g., "I'm not smart, I'm not skilled, I'm not loveable, and I'm not worthy."). These lies to yourself can limit hope and fuel your belief system.

The stories you run in your subconscious become reinforced with repetition.

Self-deception can move beyond lying to yourself. It can project positive attributes that aren't true. One form of self-deception is self-promotion: telling others we're more talented in some area of our life than we are. People often overestimate their abilities to promote self-confidence and positive feelings.[3] It's common when a person engages in self-deception for others to perceive them as being more competent than they are, falsely filling their self-esteem and social status. A new study found that 85 percent of job applicants lied on their resumés, providing evidence of how self-deception is the art of lying to yourself about your ability to manipulate others' thoughts.[4]

REFLECTION

- Are you clear on what a mind trick is? Mind tricks can be a reason why some people get caught in unpleasant emotions for years.

- Are you engaging in any at-risk behaviours that are not good for you in order to escape unwanted stress?

- Are you concerned about self-deception and how it may be negatively affecting how you experience the world?

Honesty is hard. The other ingredients in this book will help shape what you think. However, sometimes before we move forward, we need to stop engaging in behaviours that make it hard for us to think clearly. For example, a person with a substance-use disorder must first get the chemicals out of their body to have a clear mind. The next challenge is changing how they think and experience the world. Even if a person doesn't have an addiction, unhealthy habits can have a negative impact on their mind and body. Feeling controlled by a habit we don't like can create emotional strain.

Key learning for emotional well-being is keeping in mind that what we focus on will grow. When we focus on self-deception (consciously or unconsciously), it drives our negative self-talk that affects our emotional state (i.e., mood), influencing how we perceive the world and, in turn, our decisions, actions, and personal outcomes, and defines as good or bad the meaning we attach to situations. To stop self-deception, we must be clear about what we're focusing on. The influence of our social supports and life experiences (e.g., programming from people important to us, such as parents, teachers, family, and mentors) can play a significant role in creating the negative filters that limit our belief about the degree we can be happy. The peer groups we associate with are critical for our emotional well-being. If we're around people who believe and see positively, we're likely to adopt their attitude.

Microskills for Managing Self-Deception

Focus energy on what you want to think about yourself both at home and work. Leveraging your most trusted friends, mentors, or partner to obtain regular, objective, honest feedback can help keep you grounded in your strengths and gaps. Pay attention to the language you say to yourself and what others say to you, as this influences what you think about yourself. If you want to have more pleasant emotions and positive thinking, it's necessary to feed your mind with what you want it to have. Self-deception is how you try to compensate for not feeling the way you want. To stop it, be clear on how it's created from within and the environment.

Ask yourself if it's okay to deceive others and why. The human mind can play tricks on us. If we're not paying attention, our mind can tell us stories of why doing something such as exaggerating the truth is helpful. When we're aware and in tune, we can challenge ourselves by asking a simple question: "If the story I'm about to tell were reported on the front page of the newspaper, would I be okay with that?" Self-editing can be one of the best ways to mitigate the risk that self-deception can create when we start to project that false view to the world.

Be clear between confidence and character. Most of us exaggerate to make a story sound better, or we forget some fact and replace it with another that may be more favourable to the story than the original. The more we can focus on our character and become comfortable with who we are, the more likely we'll accept who we are. Learning to accept and become more content with ourselves and our station in life enhances our mental health.

Cognitive Dissonance

Self-deception can be more challenging to deal with when it involves cognitive dissonance. Cognitive dissonance is when we experience the mental strain of having two conflicting beliefs and values, creating an inconsistency between what we believe and how we behave. Cognitive dissonance is triggered when we feel psychologically uncomfortable with our thoughts (i.e., dissonance). It results in us being motivated to avoid facts and focus on making the dissonance a less negative alternative than our current reality.[5] For example, a person who tells their friends and family they want to be healthy (cognitive) might binge eat alone at night (dissonance).

Some common signs you may be struggling with cognitive dissonance:

- You feel regret for making a poor decision.

- You experience guilt after doing something.

- You attempt to justify a decision to yourself and others.

- You feel shameful about something you've done and try to hide it from others.

Before we can deal with a mind trick, it's helpful to pause and think about the ingredients required to stop. We need to know about the dopamine reward system, what unpleasant emotions really are, and the power of positive thinking and being honest with ourselves. This knowledge is not optional. We can't stop an at-risk behaviour until we're honest with ourselves and admit that what we're doing is not in our best interests. There's no magic for stopping a mind trick; it takes work. Often it will be hard, but it is doable.

18

Confronting a Mind Trick

REGARDLESS OF the root cause of an unpleasant emotion, when you get stuck in a mind trick, at-risk behaviour can result in unhealthy habits that, if not dealt with, could become serious addictions. This chapter will provide a framework for navigating at-risk behaviours. Sometimes, a person gets trapped in the regret snare because of at-risk behaviour. As you review this framework, consider it an on-demand (when needed) skill for confronting unwanted, at-risk behaviours.

This framework is grounded in a cognitive-behavioural approach (CBA). CBAs teach how to challenge negative thinking constructively to change focus and energy. When people focus on what's possible, it can positively shape their mental state. Being in the right mental state can create hope, potential, and excitement. We're happiest when we believe we can shape our emotions by initiating the ones we want.

It's so important to understand that all emotions are temporary; they come and go. However, when we worry about being sad and focus on this too often, we'll be sad and then look for a way to feel better. A critical factor for emotional well-being is accepting that we have much more control over our thoughts and emotions than we may know. The advice in this book is not therapy, nor is it intended for clinical intervention; it's for educational purposes only. However, it does have one thing in common with therapy: its success depends on what you're willing to focus on and do.

How Mind Tricks Work

A mind trick facilitates unwanted behaviours that become more reinforced the more they're practised. These behaviours are coping strategies to deal with unpleasant emotions like regret. A trigger is a reaction to a perceived negative stressor (e.g., situation). The stressor can come from a negative thought (e.g., "I'm a bad person") or interaction with the environment (e.g., your boss is not happy with your job performance). Stress triggers vary from person to person. They activate a perceived fear that drives the body's physiology, thoughts, and emotions, collectively called unwanted (bad) stress. How well we cope with unwanted stress determines our reactions (i.e., behaviours). The challenge for emotional well-being is when a trigger activates an automatic negative thought. With all negative thoughts come unpleasant emotions. The situation defines what unpleasant emotion is activated.

Here's an example:

Trigger: You believe someone has rejected you because you did something wrong.

Automatic negative thought: "I deserve what I get."

Unpleasant emotions don't drive our choice of behaviour, but they do drive behaviour. Thinking we must escape or avoid them drives at-risk behaviours to cope that may not be helpful. Whenever we experience a difference between what we *have* and what we *want*, what often comes is a wave of stress. When we experience a powerful emotion such as anxiety and worry, it can feel like the emotion is telling us what to do. It's helpful to understand and accept that emotions do not tell us what to do. They only notify us that something is not right, like a warning gauge in a car.

One common challenge for many is what we do after we experience an unwanted stressor (e.g., someone judges us in public). The stressor is also just information. The problem for many is how to react to this information. When we overreact to a stressor, it can often make the situation worse. To cope with unpleasant emotions, the problem can go beyond how we react. For example, eating to cope with stress creates the feel-good habit of using food. If we do this over and over, we can end up putting on excess body weight that can lead to other health issues. Eating when we are not hungry but to feel good (if not managed) can become an at-risk behaviour. This often happens as well with alcohol, drugs, and gambling.

At the core, the intention when looking to escape unpleasant emotions includes the following:

- **Search for relief**—Most humans seek pleasure rather than pain. It's common for a person experiencing emotional pain to want to escape it as fast as possible. The subconscious mind fires off options without judging whether they're good or bad.

- **Moment of relief**—Any at-risk behaviour chosen to change our mental state (mood and emotions) is an attempt to reduce the emotional pain. The challenge is that looking for moments of relief can result in unhealthy, at-risk behaviours becoming reinforced and anchored.

- **Changed mental state**—Any at-risk behaviour that provides a moment of relief that changes a mental state on demand can be stored as a viable future option. The experience of its benefit will define the likelihood we'll repeat it. In some cases, a behaviour that changed a state may not be filed as a future option. Taking magic mushrooms to escape emotional pain is more likely to be filed as an unwise option or deleted if it results in a "bad trip" and the emergency department.

REFLECTION

Pick one at-risk behaviour you've done in the past or are actively engaging in. By answering the following questions, you can see firsthand how an at-risk behaviour can take hold:

1 Trigger: What is one trigger that creates an urge to engage in this at-risk behaviour?

2 Emotion: What is one unpleasant emotion that comes up with this trigger?

3 Search for relief: What options come to the surface with this trigger?

4 Moment of relief: What relief does the at-risk behaviour provide?

5 Changed mental state: How does the at-risk behaviour change your mental state?

Leveraging any CBA begins with self-awareness and then accepting that you have control over your decisions. Your belief system shapes your identity and perceived self-worth. Be mindful of self-deception and cognitive dissonance, as they'll shade how you view the world and yourself if you're not aware.

What You Think about *You*

What you think about yourself matters (e.g., the extent you believe you're good enough for a job promotion you want). When the job you want is posted, you don't apply. Why? Perhaps self-doubt caused your belief about your chances of getting the job to be so low that you concluded, "There's no use applying, as I won't get it." By not trying, you strengthen the belief that you're not good enough.

Unpleasant emotions and negative thoughts are connected. Like in this example of self-doubt, the mind plays tricks. Based on a flawed belief system ("I'm not good enough to apply for this job."), the consequences of not applying are increased feelings of depression.

In Western culture, depression is becoming a bigger problem. A person depressed is three times more likely to experience death by suicide.[1] Depression co-occurs with alcohol dependence in about 80 percent of patients, and 30 to 40 percent of alcohol-dependent men and women suffer from an independent, major depressive episode during their lifetime.[2] Many depressed people use alcohol to escape emotional pain. If repeated, this use will become a psychological and physical dependency.

Please note: If you're struggling with alcohol and want to stop, discuss your situation with your medical doctor because, if you have a substance dependency, stopping without medical supervision can be lethal.

Halting At-Risk Behaviours and Negative Habits

This section is for educational purposes only. It's not meant to take the place of clinical treatment.

Hearing the truth can be hard; however, it can be a fantastic gift when we're open to it. My truth for you when it comes to stopping an at-risk behaviour that may have become an unwanted habit is there are *no shortcuts*. You must be willing and committed to doing the work. There's no escaping this fact.

REFLECTION

Knowing where you're starting can help you understand what ingredients you'll benefit from focusing more energy on.

- **How important is mental health to you?** It's helpful to pause and reflect on your core values, as they're the filters you use to make decisions. To shape your mental health, you must want to be emotionally well. Pay close attention to whether your decisions are supporting your physical and mental health. Choosing the ingredients for setting your life course can be an important foundational step.

- **How committed are you to developing positive thinking?** On a typical day, what percentage of your mood is pleasant and what percentage is unpleasant? If you're not practising positive thinking daily, you're more likely to have long periods of unpleasantness. Sadly, the default mode is negative for too many. We can modify this by changing our focus and energy to dial in on what we want to do that fuels happiness. Write down ten activities that make you happy. My list includes walking my dog, Link, teaching, creating, playing golf, boating, having coffee with a friend, spending time with family—things that make me happy because I have chosen them. I allow my mind to focus on what I want for my life rather than what I don't want. Changing our emotional state is not complex; it requires action and practice.

- **How aware are you of how unwanted habits form?** An at-risk behaviour like eating one bag of potato chips one night to cope with stress is not a problem. It becomes a problem when the person feels they're losing control of decisions and is compelled to eat a large bag of chips every night, which can move an at-risk behaviour to an unhealthy habit.

19

Prepare–Plan–Practise

THIS CHAPTER provides guidance on how to counter a mind trick, but has many applications to counter all kinds of at-risk behaviour, regardless of the unpleasant emotion driving it. Once you identify the at-risk behaviour, you can begin to engage the three-step "Prepare–Plan–Practise" approach to stop. To be successful with this microskill, you must be open and willing to reading this chapter carefully and then applying each step. Accept that this is a process and that how long it takes will depend on your situation. Think about the process versus the outcome. Success depends on making healthy decisions that prepare you to stop the old behaviour and start a new one.

Stopping a mind trick begins with a desire to learn how to feel good in a healthy way. Your success with this strategy will be influenced by how you progressed in the other ingredients. Your emotional literacy will influence your ability to tolerate some of the emotional strain that comes with shifting from an old mindset to a new one. Building in the expectation that you want to feel differently doesn't mean it will be automatic or easy.

What you focus on will determine where you land. If you want to stop a mind trick that's supporting an at-risk behaviour, you will. Keep in mind that you don't have to do this alone. If you're struggling, support and your environment can help you create the mindset to push through the challenging moments. Where you focus your attention is where you put your energy. If your attention is on being positive and how you want your future to be, this focus can help you do the work to get there, one day at a time.

Step 1: Prepare

Challenging an at-risk behaviour or unwanted habit begins with preparation. If you were going to climb Mount Everest, you wouldn't try to do it without gaining extensive experience on less lofty peaks. At a minimum, your fitness would need to be at a certain level to influence your mental state to believe you could climb the mountain. If you're struggling to breathe, you're likely to stop your training and eventually give up your quest.

There's no value in building a plan to eliminate an at-risk behaviour or unwanted habit until you are prepared mentally for the challenge. It begins with an internal desire and motivation. However, desire and motivation aren't enough. You must also be honest with yourself that changing is important because your current behaviour is not aligned with your core values for how you want to live your life. It's important to be aware of the questions you're asking yourself because they'll influence your mental state, mood, and perception of what you want to do. Your perception will determine your decisions, which will drive your behaviour and decide your outcome.

Before you begin, remind yourself of the importance of changing this behaviour. You know it's not in your long-term best interest to continue it, but to be able to stop it, you have to want to do so. Asking the following questions can convince you of the importance of changing your at-risk behaviour and that you have the knowledge and skills to now do so. The other important question to ask is, "Why now?" If you're unclear, keep asking this question until you can answer it. You'll likely not be able to stop an at-risk behaviour or unhealthy habit until you're clear on your *why*.

Answer the following questions in writing, and then read your answers out loud to yourself:

- **Life course check-in:** How is this at-risk behaviour or unwanted habit negatively affecting my life course?

- **Unpleasant emotions:** How confident am I in my ability to regulate unpleasant emotions? Stopping an at-risk behaviour or an unwanted habit requires managing unpleasant emotions with courage and tolerance.

- **Positive thoughts:** How confident am I in my ability to have more positive thoughts than negative? What positive-thought microskills am I practising daily? Through focus and daily practice, you can learn to challenge unwanted, negative thoughts and replace them with neutral or positive thoughts. Your belief system is where your automatic, subconscious thoughts come from. Pay attention to what you say to yourself, as that's what you'll believe to be true.

- **Brain:** How well do I understand how my brain works and how it influences my at-risk behaviour?

- **Habit formation:** Do I understand how my habit was formed? Do I acknowledge the role of the dopamine reward system in anchoring this habit?

- **Safety:** Am I confident that it's safe for me to stop my at-risk behaviour alone? If you're unsure and not seeking professional support, it's okay. If you're involved in an at-risk behaviour such as addiction or self-harm (e.g., cutting), it's prudent to consult a mental health professional or medical doctor and essential if you have a substance dependency.

- **Recruit supports:** What kind of supports do I need (e.g., emotional, motivational, accountability)? When stopping an at-risk behaviour or breaking an unwanted habit, it's helpful to recruit friends or professionals to provide emotional support and hold you accountable. They can also provide motivation and encouragement. Be clear on what you expect from your support system and set boundaries. For example, it's not realistic to expect a peer to provide you with psychological counselling. Be mindful that you don't put too much on your supporters. Look to them for encouragement and acknowledgement that will provide you with some accountability. In the end, accountability must fall with you. It's your life.

Step 2: Plan

The next step is planning. Use the following points to frame your plan to stop an old behaviour and start a new one.

Lock in your start date: Lock in the date when you'll begin your process to stop this at-risk behaviour or unwanted habit.

Make a triggers inventory: While in a calm state, you can think much more clearly than under stress. A part of your planning is to identify triggers associated with the at-risk behaviour or unwanted habit. What do you believe are internal and external triggers, and why? Notice when there's a stress trigger that overwhelms your brain. The stress trigger (e.g., perceived failure) fires off the need to curb emotional pain. The source of stress, such as a failure, maybe the trigger in this case. Naming triggers is important so you can prepare for and anticipate them.

Determine replacement behaviour: Now that you've decided to stop a behaviour, plan what activities you'll replace it with. Metaphorically consider the at-risk behaviour or unwanted habit you want to stop as if it's a cracked decoration sitting on your Christmas tree. It's not desirable and is something you want to replace. If you take the ornament off the tree, you must add a new one to fill the space.

The main character in my book *The Coping Crisis* is Sam, a client who had a habit of night snacking.[1] Potato chips were a favourite food he consumed for hours each night as he sat in front of a TV. Sam discovered how to replace night snacking with physical activity and expanded his social life by engaging in volunteer activities. Moving forward with stopping an at-risk behaviour or unwanted habit comes down to replacing it with something more desirable and healthier.

REFLECTION

- You'll never forget how to engage in an old, at-risk behaviour or unwanted habit. Whether it's days, weeks, months, or years later, there may be some change in your life that causes you to become overwhelmed and slip back into an old behaviour. Slips happen, and the key is not to judge yourself. Forgive yourself quickly and get back on track. We often lapse because we lose focus, and an old or new trigger initiates an old thinking and behaviour pattern.

- Slips don't need to become full relapses; they're nothing more than mistakes. It's helpful to focus on what you can learn from a mistake, not how it defines you. Practising self-compassion helps you learn from your mistake, which is at the core of the magic of regret.

Develop urge resistance: Moving past an at-risk behaviour requires learning how to manage cues, triggers, and physiological urges. Urges can feel intense, but we can learn to resist them through focus and intention because when we don't buy into them, they decrease, fade, and eventually go away. To curb an urge, strengthen your ability to delay gratification and an immediate reward for longer-term personal gain (i.e., health). For example, the potato chips taste delicious now, and not eating them is difficult. But delaying gratification will create space for new behaviours and habits to form and eventually flourish.

Success begins with leveraging your self-control to resist the urge for gratification, a critical step in stopping an at-risk behaviour or an unwanted habit. Typically, you'll notice the frequency, duration, and intensity of urges are at their strongest when you first decide to stop a behaviour or habit. Resisting them can be challenging, as there's a strong reward loop that will need some time to be broken. However, urges decline when not reinforced.

To overcome an urge, mentally practise what you'll do when you experience it. Anticipate it, focus on staying calm, know it will pass, and understand that urges don't make you do anything; they're only suggestions. They can trick a person into thinking they must give in to them, but they're temporary and will pass if you ignore them. Amos Tversky and Daniel Kahneman developed prospect theory, which suggests that humans tend to make quick decisions that are often not optimal.[2] Tversky and Kahneman teach that humans take risks based on their context of a situation or life challenge. For example, for each of the following two options, would you pick A or B, and why?

Option 1:
A A sure win of $250, versus
B A 25 percent chance to win $1,000 and a 75 percent chance to win nothing

Option 2:
A A sure loss of $750, versus
B A 75 percent chance to lose $1,000 and a 25 percent chance to lose nothing

Tversky and Kahneman's research found that what people will do is often based on how the choice is framed.[3] Most will pick A in Option 1 because it's riskless. In Option 2, they'll choose B because, even though they can lose more, it appears less risky. Why? The theory is based on the notion that humans dislike losses more than equal gains. When it comes to at-risk behaviour, the loss of a decision that creates an opportunity for new pleasure can be difficult when a solid foundation is not in place (e.g., set life course, support systems, emotional literacy, and positive thinking).

Stopping an at-risk behaviour or unwanted habit can be challenging and confusing because often the replacement behaviour doesn't provide the same immediate symptom relief. It usually takes time for the benefit of a new behaviour to be recognized. A basic tenet of behavioural economics is humans often make decisions based on their perceived value at the time. In the moment, it's easier to prioritize behaviours that ease pain and feel good now (eating a bag of potato chips) over ones that will help us avoid pain and feel good in the future (*not* eating a bag of potato chips). Little wonder so many people struggle, as they're motivated more by pain than by pleasure. Discovering delayed gratification can be an opportunity to flip this script.

Gamification: Self-control creates a bridge and space for new habits to form and become automatic. It's not a long-term success strategy. You can amplify your self-control by adding some gamification to provide extra motivation. For example, you want to stop night snacking. You decide for your game that you will add a consequence if you break your pact with yourself: if you eat potato chips, you'll pay an accountability fine (e.g., do a task you don't enjoy). This stimulus-response approach can train your brain to think that the short-term benefits of potato chips are too expensive. This mindset can help you create the required repetitions for the replacement behaviour to take hold and put the old, at-risk behaviour or unwanted habit in a box. It's also helpful to add a positive reward, such as treating yourself to a movie for hitting a milestone of one week with no potato chips.

Microskills for Maturing Delayed Gratification

One way to mature delayed gratification is to practise emotional agility: your level of comfort in tolerating your inner thoughts in a non-judgemental and intentional manner.[4]

Base your decisions on your core health value. It's much easier to resist unhealthy temptations when you're clear on how they're not good for your health or aligned with what you want. Stopping at-risk behaviours or unwanted habits begins with a desire based on a commitment to your health value. Your health value is a filter that influences your day-to-day decisions and motivation to challenge urges and engage in new, healthy behaviours that can, in time, bring positive benefits.

Emotional agility anchors the notion that it's unrealistic to expect you to have 100 percent control over unpleasant emotions. Unpleasant emotions are transient and don't define how you're doing. You have that choice when you discover that emotions are gauges and don't necessarily equal truth or reality.

Practise being an observer, instead of reacting to unpleasant emotions, to help you move through and past urges. Accept that you'll never omit all unpleasant emotions. However, with focus and mindfulness, you can learn to accept that they happen and discover that you don't have to react to them. When you learn to accept unpleasant emotions as the same as positive emotions, it weakens their control over you and your urgency to react.

Step 3: Practise

Accepting that failure is a normal part of the process may not be motivating but is reality. There's no such thing as perfection. Shaming yourself when you spill milk does nothing to clean up the mess. To move forward, you must first clean up the spill, then try again by getting another glass of milk. Slips happen for many reasons, such as losing focus or a life distraction. They don't have to define your success and have nothing to do with being weak or uncommitted. They happen because old programming is not fully secured in a box, and the new programming's value is not fully integrated.

Practising is about learning not to allow the stress from the triggers make you feel like you must react. You can learn how to make better choices by developing your tolerance to stress, because you understand the choices are what matters. With practice, you can develop more stress tolerance to triggers. Research based on stress inoculation has found that intentional practice to cope with stressful situations can help you deal with them successfully.[5] Surgeons and Navy SEALs are trained by inducing stress so they can learn how to tolerate it. Stopping a behaviour is a process, not an event. Self-compassion is a key ingredient.

Go Live: Installing New Healthy Behaviours and Habits

One ingredient for success is being more aware of your brain's ability to rewire through neuroplasticity. Through repetition and practice, the brain can create new neural pathways. There are no magic shortcuts. Learning new behaviours takes energy, repetition, and time. It can take more than two hundred days to make a new behaviour become an automatic habit. Committing to the process, not the finish line, will help you achieve your desired outcome. New habits will evolve, provided you're intentional and aware.

Game Plan for Anchoring a New Habit

Framing your game plan to stop old behaviours and replace them with new, healthy behaviours requires action. This game plan's purpose is to frame action.

PLANNING WORKSHEET

My trigger (e.g., work demands):

_____

_____

_____

Behaviour I want to stop (e.g., eating potato chips):

_____

_____

_____

Replacement behaviour (e.g., in-vivo meditation):

_____

_____

_____

DAILY LOG

Urge to engage in old behaviour (high/medium/low):

_____

Ability to perceive benefits of new behaviour
(high/medium/low):

_____

Note:

- If you're not sure you can cope with an at-risk behaviour, please consult a mental health professional.

- If you're concerned about your daily alcohol intake, consult with your medical doctor on the best course of action before stopping.

Epilogue
Baking Your Emotional Well-Being Plan

THIS BOOK'S end goal is to help people cope with regret better. It can also help reduce the time a person spends in unpleasant emotions that can negatively impact emotional well-being. After reading each chapter, you now can decide what ingredients and parts you will focus on first. For example, if you're emotionally upset, you may want to focus on emotional regulation before setting a life course.

You can't build a house overnight; you do it step by step. As much as you may be looking for quick fixes, there are no shortcuts. If you want to develop your emotional well-being, spend less time in unpleasant emotions, and live a life with no regrets, you need to do the work, period. You'll need to work at it for months, no different than if you decided to lose thirty pounds. It's easy to be unhappy. It's harder to find happiness, since it requires owning our behaviour.

The key to developing emotional well-being is focusing on the process, not the outcome. You'll discover the benefits of daily intention and focus and clearing out negative thoughts through practice. Instead of reacting or running away from unpleasant emotions, you'll be making decisions based on values, being mindful of your reputation and committed to living with no regrets.

Go slow and pick one or two things a month to focus on. When dealing with emotional well-being, often less is more. A month goes by fast when you have purpose and personal goals. On the first of each month, set your goals for that month. Leverage the book for ideas as to what you will do next or to re-explore an idea, as you may forget some things. This is why I suggest using this book as a resource. If you've marked up the book, you can use your marks as interest guideposts to explore, review, and consider.

Success won't be defined by how much you think. It will be determined by how you influence your sense of overall emotional well-being. We all have busy lives. Adding a new focus means dedicating energy, time, and attention. Emotional well-being transformation is not a spectator sport; it requires conviction and focus on the long game.

Baking Your Plan

First, determine your baseline for the month. For each ingredient, consider where you think and feel you are today. Each month, review how you think and feel about each ingredient to set your priority focus for the month.

1   Realization
(e.g., My brain is a powerful tool. I want to learn about how to navigate it better.)

_____

_____

2 Realignment

(e.g., Creating and following a life course is a priority for me.)

_____

_____

3 Reputation

(e.g., How I show up and manage my emotions influence my reputation.)

_____

_____

4 Reserves

(e.g., Training my brain to be more positive is of benefit to me, influencing my beliefs and mental state.)

_____

_____

5 Reset

(e.g., I'm concerned about an at-risk behaviour/unwanted habit that now requires my attention.)

_____

_____

Next, based on the work from the above exercise, decide what you'll focus on over the next thirty days. Emotional well-being is not a sprint, it's a marathon, so pick no more than two or three focus areas each month. Be specific about what you'll do. For each focus area, be clear on *why* you want to deal with it, *what* you will do *when*, and *how* you will define success. The following is a sample monthly plan.

Monthly Emotional Well-Being Plan

Focus area #1: Be honest with myself about what regrets I have.

Ingredient: Reality

Why am I picking this focus? I want to live my life with no regrets. The only way to do so is to explore my regrets, not hide from them.

What will I do to achieve this goal, and when? I will complete the regret inventory within the next two weeks.

How will I define success? I will have created my regret inventory and picked at least one regret I want to confront.

What is the next action? I will explore the regret I picked within the context of the regret snare and then identify opportunities and actions to move past it.

Keep top of mind that change is a process and will not happen overnight, so be patient. This self-tolerance can help create space and focus on your desired outcomes. Your daily actions within the plan will play a critical role in reaching those outcomes and improving your overall emotional well-being.

In Closing

I'm not hopeful there will be a pill that creates emotional well-being in my lifetime. It seems to me that we'll all be responsible for figuring out how to master it.

Monks, philosophers, academic scholars, spiritual leaders, psychiatrists, psychologists, counsellors, social workers, and other professionals who help humans navigate the four inches between the ears all agree that achieving emotional well-being requires focus, intention, and action. We're the captains responsible for our emotional well-being; we can't outsource it. One joy in my work is when a person like you discovers they can learn to positively impact their emotional well-being through their daily choices and actions.

I wish you an insightful, emotional well-being journey.

All the best.

DR. BILL HOWATT

Acknowledgements

COVID-19 HAS awoken me to take action and learn how to better live my life with no regrets.

I am blessed to have care and support from friends, family, and my brothers Robbie and Peter. Special friends who helped me get through the past year are Sophie, Richie, Brad, Patty, Tara, Wendy, Alex, and Chris.

Thank you to Amanda Lewis and Emily Schultz, as well as the team at Page Two, who have been very good to me... and patient!

Perhaps my biggest source of positive energy comes from my forty-pound eighteen-month-old miniature English bulldog, Link. He has provided me with much guidance and encouragement on the value of living in the moment. Though some may say he is just a dog, for me, he is my best buddy.

Appendix A
Stress-Load Monitor

T HERE ARE two types of stress. Eustress is good stress. The more commonly known bad stress is called distress. Stress occurs when we have a difference between what we want and what we have. The challenge with stress is it takes energy and can quickly drain our resources. When we create a perception that we can't cope, we're at significant risk, which is why it's helpful to monitor our weekly stress load and, if it's higher than we'd like, take action. The longer we experience distress, the greater the risk to our health. Research shows that stress kills when it's ignored. It can also affect physical health (e.g., ulcers, heart attack, and stroke) and mental health (e.g., anxiety and depression).

One challenge with stress is that it can negatively impact decision making, goal-setting, and impulse control when it becomes chronic. Therefore, it's helpful to get a baseline on your stress level and track it weekly to monitor or evaluate whether the microdecisions and behaviours you're engaging in are helping or hurting you.

On a scale of 1 (strongly disagree) to 5 (strongly agree), rate how much you agree with each of the following statements regarding your experience over the past seven days, then total your score to determine your risk level:

I'm struggling financially. ____

I'm not getting along with my partner, family, or friends. ____

I'm struggling to keep up with the demands of home and work.____

When I think about the people I work with, I get tense. ____

It feels like my stress level is high each day. ____

At the end of each day, I physically crash because of all the pressure and stress. ____

When I think about my current job, it's indeed painful. ____

I'm in constant conflict with people at home or work. ____

When I feel stressed, I engage in harmful actions to feel good (e.g., drinking, eating, drugs, avoiding situations, etc.). ____

I'm not coping well with my current stress load. ____

I'm tense about failing at work and losing my job. ____

I proactively engage in activities daily to prepare me to manage life stress (e.g., physical fitness, meditation, hobbies, etc.). ____

TOTAL SCORE: ____

This is not a clinical measure or diagnostic tool; it's meant to be only a screening tool.

Potential Risk Levels

12–15: Low Risk

This score suggests that you appear to be managing your life stress well, increasing your ability to take on more challenges. Do you agree with this evaluation? If you do, are you clear on why you're having low stress and what you're doing well that supports your ability to cope or have low stress? It's beneficial to reinforce your daily habits and decisions that help reduce your risk of stress or process and cope with it. There's no escaping life and the challenges that come with it. Most of us have some degree of stress we need to process daily or weekly.

16–25: Low to Moderate Risk

This score suggests that, for the most part, you're doing okay dealing with your stress. However, having one area of your life creating stress can become a problem area if ignored and allowed to grow. Be critical, pay attention to what's stressing you out, and evaluate what you can do to reduce your stress load. You always have a choice. Often, the challenge to move past some stressors is whether you're ready to face the consequences. Step one is awareness: pay attention to what you're thinking and feeling. The next step is accountability. You own your behaviour and choices. Getting rid of some stress in your life often requires deciding to do something and owning the consequences. The next step is making an action plan. If you know what to do, set your plan and timeline and measure your success weekly. If you're unsure, ask for support and guidance from a trusted peer, partner, family member or to get a frame of reference of where to start. The goal is to get ahead of stress before it negatively impacts your health, relationships, work, and life.

26–60: Moderate to High Risk

This score suggests that you could benefit from reducing your stress level before it becomes more problematic. You're likely experiencing some of the symptoms listed below. The only way to stop stress is to act. If you don't have insight into what you can do to improve your stress level, talk to a trusted peer or an employee and family assistance representative to get some guidance. As well, evaluate your coping skills regarding gaps. Coping is a trainable skill, and with support, you can learn more skills to help you solve your current challenges so you can make better decisions for your long-term health.

Signs and Symptoms of Stress

Physical

- Back pain
- Chronic illness/flu or colds
- Constipation
- Dizziness or fainting
- Dry mouth
- Excessive perspiration
- Headaches
- High blood pressure
- Indigestion/nausea
- Insomnia or fatigue
- Muscle aches or spasms
- Over/undereating
- Pounding heart
- Sexual dysfunction
- Shortness of breath
- Skin rashes
- Ulcers/diarrhea

Psychological

- Anger
- Anxiety
- Apathy
- Boredom
- Depression
- Fatigue
- Fear of death
- Frustration
- Guilt
- Hopelessness
- Hostility
- Impatience
- Inability to concentrate
- Irritability
- Restlessness

Behavioural

- Biting lips
- Child/spousal abuse
- Drug and/or alcohol abuse
- Foot tapping
- Grinding teeth
- Impulsive actions
- Increased smoking
- Isolating from family and friends
- Moving in tense, jerky ways
- Nervous tics
- Trembling hands
- Overreacting
- Rapid mood swings
- Stuttering
- Swearing
- Touching hair, ears, or nose

Appendix B
Happiness IQ Quick Screen

William Howatt PhD, EdD

HOW HAPPY are you on a typical day? Watching Matthew McConaughey's 2014 Oscars acceptance speech inspired me to develop this tool. He shared what appeared to be a powerful formula and call to action for happiness: "What do you look up to? What do you look forward to? What do you chase?" Brilliant advice! People who focus on being happy are 50 percent less likely to have heart attacks or catch the flu and are more likely to live a longer and healthier life. Neuroscience shows that people's answers about their level of happiness correlate with activity in the part of the brain where the feeling of happiness is.[1] It's clear that the more happy thoughts you have, the more likely you will report yourself as being a happy person. One effective defence for life stress is the creation of internal happiness.

Based on a typical day, rate on a scale of 1 (strongly disagree) to 5 (strongly agree) how you would respond to the following statements, then total your score to determine your happiness IQ:

Overall, my life is what I want it to be. ____

I get up every day with a purpose. ____

I have achieved what I want to at this point in my life. ____

If I could redo my life, there's not much I would change. ____

I'm a cheerful person. ____

My personal relationships are wonderful. ____

TOTAL SCORE: ____

This is not a clinical measure or diagnostic tool; it's meant to be only a screening tool.

Happiness IQ

6–18: Sorry, You're not Happy

Ed Diener reported that, in general, people are happy if they think they're happy; you're the best judge of whether you're happy.[2] At this level, you're not as happy as you want to be or could be. Figure out your barriers to happiness. If you can't do this alone, get some help. We all have the potential to be happier, but it takes action. Be mindful that many mental health conditions can sneak up on people who are worried, depressed, or feel their life is not under control.

19–23: You're Okay—but Okay Is Not Happy

We know that there's no correlation between happiness and money, but there is between happiness and relationships. Every happy relationship you have tends to improve your happiness by 9 percent. Other suggestions for getting more happiness in your life include exercising, getting enough sleep, going outside, volunteering, meditating, and practising gratitude.[3]

24–30: You're Happy

Congratulations, you've found a path many seek. About one in three people reports they're happy. But happiness is subjective and can change from moment to moment. The pillars of happiness are self-acceptance, relationships, health, social contribution, and feeling like you're making a difference. To insulate your happiness, be mindful of your habits and keep giving to others; this gift keeps giving back.

Appendix C
Optimism Quick Screen

© 2014 William Howatt PhD, EdD

W E ALL fall on a continuum from optimism to pessimism. Optimistic people see the glass as half-full, while pessimistic people see it half-empty. Optimism has a positive effect on mental and physical health.[1] A person who has an optimistic view of the world sees more positives and opportunities. A pessimistic person is negative, constantly feels challenged, and often acts as if the world is out to get them. Sadly, pessimistic people, often without knowing, are creating a self-fulfilling prophecy. The good news is that pessimistic people can, through coping-skills training, learn to be more optimistic.

The purpose of this screen is to help you evaluate where you fit on the continuum. Based on a typical day, rate on a scale of 1 (strongly disagree) to 5 (strongly agree) how true the statements are, then total your score. The higher your score, the more optimistic you are; the lower your score, the higher your probability of pessimism.

I find it easy to take time to relax and enjoy the day. ____

I feel good about my future. ____

In the most challenging times, I tend to think things will work out fine. ____

I rarely believe things are going to go wrong for me. ____

I typically believe that if I work hard, I will get what I focus on.____

I believe the next ninety days will be excellent. ____

I daily notice more positives than negatives. ____

I daily expect more good things than bad will happen. ____

TOTAL SCORE: ____

This is not a clinical screen; it's for educational purposes only.

Potential Pessimism Level

8-18: Tend to Be More Pessimistic

If you fall in this range, the first question is: Would you like to be more optimistic? If so, you can benefit from coping skills training. If you're very low in this range, it's worth exploring your score with a mental health professional to rule out any issues that may be contributing to your current view of the world. The good news is that there are things you can do to learn to be more optimistic. If you're unsure where to start and want to feel better, talk with a mental health professional.

19-25: Can Flip-Flop between Feeling Pessimistic and Optimistic

Many people find themselves in this range. How they deal with stress influences how they feel about their future. It's important to remember that thoughts are not our reality. What we do with our thoughts defines our reality. People who find themselves in this category and have periods when they're optimistic, followed by periods of feeling pessimistic, benefit from focusing on developing their coping skills (e.g., taking coping-skills or mindfulness training). If you're unsure where to start, talk to someone trained in mental health. This field is growing; more people are looking to develop this skill set.

26-40: Tend to Be More Optimistic

This is a wonderful way to see the world for yourself and others around you. Keep doing what you're doing that's working, and stay in tune with why you're optimistic about your future. Make an effort and don't take it for granted. Sometimes, optimistic people start to associate with negative, energy-draining people. Without their knowing it, this interaction can influence their view of the world and make them more negative. Pay attention to your environment and be aware that you always have control over your thinking and behaviours. This side of the continuum on average is a much more peaceful and happier place to be.

Notes

Introduction

1 Colleen Saffrey, Amy Summerville, and Neal J. Roese, "Praise for Regret: People Value Regret above Other Negative Emotions," *Motivation and Emotion* 32, no. 1 (2008): 46–54, doi.org/10.1007/s11031-008-9082-4.

2 Elaine Mead, "What Are Negative Emotions and How to Control Them?" Positive Psychology, positivepsychology.com/negative-emotions.

3 Stephen R. Covey, *The 7 Habits of Highly Effective People* (New York: Simon & Schuster, 2020).

4 "Global Burden of Mental Disorders and the Need for a Comprehensive, Coordinated Response from Health and Social Sectors at the Country Level," World Health Organization, December 1, 2011, apps.who.int/gb/ebwha/pdf_files/EB130/B130_9-en.pdf.

5 Bill Howatt, *Stop Hiding and Start Living: How to Say F-it to Fear and Develop Mental Fitness* (Vancouver: Page Two, 2020).

6 Samantha K. Brooks et al., "The Psychological Impact of Quarantine and How to Reduce It: Rapid Review of the Evidence," *Lancet* 395, no. 10227 (2020): 912–920, doi.org/10.1016/S0140-6736(20)30460-8.

7 Bill Howatt, *The Cure for Loneliness: How to Feel Connected and Escape Isolation* (Vancouver: Page Two, 2021).

8 "Average Hours per Day Spent in Selected Activities by Employment Status and Sex, 2019 Annual Averages," U.S. Bureau of Labor Statistics, bls.gov/charts/american-time-use/activity-by-emp.htm.

9 Seph Fontane Pennock, "Who Is Martin Seligman and What Does He Do?" Positive Psychology, positivepsychology.com/who-is-martin-seligman.

10 Quoted in Courtney E. Ackerman, "Flourishing in Positive Psychology: Definition + 8 Practical Tips," Positive Psychology, positivepsychology.com/flourishing.

Chapter 1: What Is Regret?

1 Thomas Gilovich, Ranxiao Frances Wang, Dennis Regan, and Sadafumi Nishina, "Regrets of Action and Inaction across Cultures," *Journal of Cross-Cultural Psychology* 34, no. 1 (2003): 61–71, doi.org/10.1177/0022022102239155.

2 Terry Connolly and Marcel Zeelenberg, "Regret in Decision Making," *Current Directions in Psychological Science* 11, no. 6 (2002): 212–216, doi.org/10.1111/1467-8721.00203.

3 "Regret," Emotion Typology, emotiontypology.com/negative_emotion/regret.

4 Michael W. Morris and Paul C. Moore, "The Lessons We (Don't) Learn: Counterfactual Thinking and Organizational Accountability after a Close Call," *Administrative Science Quarterly* 45, no. 4 (2000): 737–765, doi.org/10.2307/2667018.

5 Daniel Kahneman and Amos Tversky, "The Simulation Heuristic," in *Judgment under Uncertainty: Heuristics and Biases*, edited by Daniel Kahneman, Paul Slovic, and Amos Tversky (New York: Cambridge University Press, 1982): 201–8.

6 Eric van Dijk and Marcel Zeelenberg, "On the Psychology of 'If Only': Regret and the Comparison between Factual and Counterfactual Outcomes," *Organizational Behavior and Human Decision Processes* 97, no. 2 (2005): 152–160, doi.org/10.1016/j.obhdp.2005.04.001.

7 Kendra Cherry, "What Are Heuristics?" Verywell Mind, February 13, 2022, verywellmind.com/what-is-a-heuristic-2795235.

8 Kendra Cherry, "How Hindsight Bias Affects How We View the Past," Verywell Mind, May 6, 2020, verywellmind.com/what-is-a-hindsight-bias-2795236.

9 Marcel Zeelenberg et al., "Emotional Reactions to the Outcomes of Decisions: The Role of Counterfactual Thought in the Experience of Regret and Disappointment," *Organizational Behavior and Human Decision Processes* 75, no. 2 (1998): 117–41, doi.org/10.1006/obhd.1998.2784.

10   Richard B. Joelson, "Locus of Control," *Psychology Today*, August 2, 2017, psychologytoday.com/ca/blog/moments-matter/201708/locus-control.

11   Anna D. Rowe and Julie Fitness, "Understanding the Role of Negative Emotions in Adult Learning and Achievement: A Social Functional Perspective," *Behavioral Sciences* 8, no. 2 (2018): 27, doi.org/10.3390/bs8020027.

12   Christian Jarret, "We Are Haunted More by Regrets about Not Becoming the Person We Wanted to Be, than Not Becoming the Person We Were Expected to Be," Research Digest, British Psychological Society, May 3, 2018, digest.bps.org.uk/2018/05/03/we-are-haunted-more-by-regrets-about-not-becoming-the-person-we-wanted-to-be-than-about-not-becoming-the-person-we-were-expected-to-be.

13   Shai Davidai and Thomas Gilovich, "The Ideal Road Not Taken: The Self-Discrepancies Involved in People's Most Enduring Regrets," *Emotion* 18, no. 3 (2018): 439–52, doi.org/10.1037/emo0000326.

14   Vanessa Van Edwards, "Regret: How to Diagnose and Overcome Your Great Regrets," Science of People, scienceofpeople.com/regret.

15   Moya Sarner, "Regret Can Seriously Damage Your Mental Health—Here's How to Leave It Behind," *Guardian*, June 27, 2019, theguardian.com/lifeandstyle/2019/jun/27/regret-can-seriously-damage-your-mental-health-heres-how-to-leave-it-behind.

16   Vered Murgraff et al., "Regret Is What You Get: The Effects of Manipulating Anticipated Affect and Time Perspective on Risky Single-Occasion Drinking," *Alcohol and Alcoholism* 34, no. 4 (1999): 590–600, doi.org/10.1093/alcalc/34.4.590.

Chapter 2: Regret Check-In

1   Malcolm Gladwell, *Blink: The Power of Thinking without Thinking* (New York: Back Bay Books, 2006).

2   Neal J. Roese and Amy Summerville, "What We Regret Most... and Why," *Personality and Social Psychology Bulletin* 31, no. 9 (2005): 1273–85, doi.org/10.1177/0146167205274693

3   Van Edwards, "Regret: How to Diagnose and Overcome Your Great Regrets."

4   Kendra Cherry, "An Overview of the Zeigarnik Effect and Memory," Verywell Mind, July 4, 2021, verywellmind.com/zeigarnik-effect-memory-overview-4175150.

Chapter 3: The Regret Snare

1   William Glasser, *Choice Theory: A New Psychology of Personal Freedom* (New York: HarperPerennial, 1999).
2   Alan Watts, *The Wisdom of Insecurity: A Message for an Age of Anxiety* (New York: Vintage, 2011).
3   Hannah Faye Chua et al., "Decision-related Loss: Regret and Disappointment," *Neuroimage* 47, no. 4 (2009): 2031–40, doi. org/10.1016/j.neuroimage.2009.06.006.

Chapter 4: A Gift or a Curse: You Decide

1   Jay Shetty, *Think Like a Monk: Train Your Mind for Peace and Purpose Every Day* (New York: Simon & Schuster, 2020).
2   Shoba Sreenivasan and Linda E. Weinberger, "What to Do with Feelings of Regret," *Psychology Today*, November 14, 2018, psychologytoday.com/ca/blog/emotional-nourishment/201811/ what-do-feelings-regret.
3   Melanie Greenberg, "The Psychology of Regret," *Psychology Today*, May 16, 2012, psychologytoday.com/ca/blog/ the-mindful-self-express/201205/the-psychology-regret.
4   Neal J. Roese, "Counterfactual Thinking," *Psychological Bulletin* 121, no. 1 (1997): 133–48, doi.org/10.1037/0033-2909.121.1.133.

Chapter 5: Why Knowing about the Brain Matters

1   Carmen Sandi, "Stress and Cognition," *WIREs Cognitive Science* 4, no. 3 (2013): 245–61, doi.org/10.1002/wcs.1222.
2   Nico H. Frijda, "The Psychologists' Point of View," in *Handbook of Emotions*, 2nd ed., ed. Michael Lewis and Jeannette M. Haviland-Jones (New York: Guilford Press, 2000): 59–74.
3   Lis Nielsen and Alfred W. Kaszniak, "Conceptual, Theoretical, and Methodological Issues in Inferring Subjective Emotion Experience: Recommendations for Researchers," in *Handbook of Emotion Elicitation and Assessment*, ed. James A. Coan and John J.B. Allen (Oxford: Oxford University Press, 2007), 361–75.
4   "How Does the Body Use Serotonin?" Endocrine Society, endocrine.org/patient-engagement/endocrine-library/ hormones-and-endocrine-function/brain-hormones.
5   Paul R. Albert and Chawki Benkelfat, "The Neurobiology of Depression: Revisiting the Serotonin Hypothesis," *Philosophical*

Transactions of the Royal Society B: Biological Sciences 368, no. 1615 (2013): 20120535, doi.org/10.1098/rstb.2012.0535.

6 Susanne Babbel, "The Connections between Emotional Stress, Trauma, and Physical Pain," *Psychology Today*, April 8, 2010, psychologytoday.com/ca/blog/somatic-psychology/201004/ the-connections-between-emotional-stress-trauma-and-physical-pain.

7 Christina Kelley, Bongshin Lee, and Lauren Wilcox, "Self-Tracking for Mental Wellness: Understanding Expert Perspectives and Student Experiences," *Proceedings of the SIGCHI Conference on Human Factors in Computing Systems* (2017): 629–41, doi. org/10.1145/3025453.3025750.

Chapter 6: Five Facts You May Not Know about Your Brain

1 Robby Berman, "New Study Suggests We Have 6,200 Thoughts Every Day," Big Think, July 16, 2020, bigthink.com/mind-brain/ how-many-thoughts-per-day.

2 Prakhar Verma, "Destroy Negativity From Your Mind With This Simple Exercise," Medium, November 27, 2017, medium.com/ the-mission/a-practical-hack-to-combat-negative-thoughts-in-2-minutes-or-less-cc3d1bddb3af.

3 Jon Kabat-Zinn, Guided Mindfulness Meditation, mindfulnesscds.com.

4 Matthew A. Killingsworth and Daniel T. Gilbert, "A Wandering Mind Is an Unhappy Mind," *Science* 330, no. 6006 (2010): 932, doi.org/10.1126/science.1192439.

5 Arno Slabbinck, "The Brain's Default Mode: What Is It and Why Meditation Is the Antidote," Medium, September 23, 2019, medium.com/swlh/the-brains-default-mode-what-is-it-and-why-meditation-is-the-antidote-d0408ab989d6.

6 Steven Kotler, "The Science of Peak Human Performance," *Time*, April 30, 2014, time.com/56809/ the-science-of-peak-human-performance.

7 Leo Babauta, "9 Steps to Achieving Flow (and Happiness) in Your Work," Zen Habits, zenhabits.net/ guide-to-achieving-flow-and-happiness-in-your-work.

8 Society for Personality and Social Psychology, "How We Form Habits, Change Existing Ones," ScienceDaily, August 8, 2014, sciencedaily.com/releases/2014/08/140808111931.htm.

9   Carol A. Seger and Brian J. Spiering, "A Critical Review of Habit Learning and the Basal Ganglia," *Frontiers in System Neuroscience* 5 (2011): 66, doi.org/10.3389/fnsys.2011.00066.

10 Marks & Spencer, *Autopilot Britain*, corporate.marksandspencer.com/documents/reports-results-and-publications/autopilot-britain-whitepaper.pdf.

11 Gustavo Razzetti, "How to Stop Living Life on Autopilot," *Psychology Today*, November 1, 2018, psychologytoday.com/ca/blog/the-adaptive-mind/201811/how-stop-living-life-autopilot.

12 Manda Mahoney, "The Subconscious Mind of the Consumer (And How To Reach It)," Working Knowledge, Harvard Business School, January 13, 2003, hbswk.hbs.edu/item/the-subconscious-mind-of-the-consumer-and-how-to-reach-it.

13 Bruce Lipton, *The Biology of Belief: Unleashing the Power of Consciousness, Matter, and Miracles* (Carlsbad, CA: Hay House, 2015).

14 Richard S. Lazarus, *Emotion and Adaptation* (New York: Oxford University Press, 1991).

15 Graham Loomes and Robert Sugden, "Regret Theory: An Alternative Theory of Rational Choice under Uncertainty," *Economic Journal* 92 (1982): 805–24, doi.org/10.2307/2232669.

16 J.W. Pennebaker, "Putting Stress into Words: Health, Linguistic, and Therapeutic Implications," *Behaviour Research and Therapy* 31, no. 6 (1993): 539–48, doi.org/10.1016/0005-7967(93)90105-4.

17 Daniel Kahneman, *Thinking, Fast and Slow* (New York: Farrar, Straus and Giroux, 2011).

18 Amos Tversky and Daniel Kahneman, "Judgment Under Uncertainty: Heuristics and Biases," *Science* 185, no. 4157 (1974): 1124–31, doi.org/10.1126/science.185.4157.1124.

19 Catherine Hambley, "Avoid Cognitive Biases in Decision-Making," Physicians Practice, June 27, 2018, physicianspractice.com/view/avoiding-cognitive-biases-decision-making.

Chapter 7: Still More Facts about Your Brain

1   Amy Morin, "10 Thinking Errors That Will Crush Your Mental Strength," *Psychology Today*, January 24, 2015, psychologytoday.com/ca/blog/what-mentally-strong-people-dont-do/201501/10-thinking-errors-will-crush-your-mental-strength.

2   Aaron T. Beck, *Cognitive Therapy and the Emotional Disorders* (Oxford: International Universities Press, 1976).

3   David D. Burns, *Feeling Good: The New Mood Therapy* (New York: Morrow, 1980).

4   David A. Clark and Aaron T. Beck, *Cognitive Therapy of Anxiety Disorders: Science and Practice* (New York: Guilford Press, 2010).

5   Sue Johnson, *Hold Me Tight: Seven Conversations for a Lifetime of Love* (New York: Little, Brown Spark, 2008).

6   Debra Campbell, "How To Rewire Your Brain to Have a Secure Attachment Style," Mindbodygreen, March 2, 2020, mindbodygreen.com/articles/how-to-develop-a-secure-attachment-style.

7   Abby Moore and Hilary Jacobs Hendel, "Anxious Attachment Style: How It Develops & How to Heal," Mindbodygreen, mindbodygreen.com/articles/anxious-attachment-style.

8   Peter Lovenheim and Kristina Hallet, "How to Be in a Relationship When You Have an Avoidant Attachment Style," Mindbodygreen, mindbodygreen.com/articles/dating-with-an-avoidant-attachment-style.

9   Kelly Gonsalves and Nicole Beurkens, "Understanding the Fearful Avoidant Attachment Style in Relationships," Mindbodygreen, mindbodygreen.com/articles/how-fearful-avoidant-attachment-style-affects-your-sex-life.

10   Harvard Health Publishing, "Can Relationships Boost Longevity and Well-Being?" Harvard Medical School, June 1, 2017, health.harvard.edu/mental-health/can-relationships-boost-longevity-and-well-being.

11   One resource I've explored and found helpful for attachment theory is the Personal Development School online course at university. personaldevelopmentschool.com.

12   J.M. Kilner and R.N. Lemon, "What We Know Currently about Mirror Neurons," *Current Biology* 23, no. 23 (2013): R1057–62, doi.org/10.1016/j.cub.2013.10.051.

13   Ryszard Praszkier, "Empathy, Mirror Neurons and SYNC," *Mind and Society* 15 (2016): 1–25, doi.org/10.1007/s11299-014-0160-x.

14   Mark Goulston, *Just Listen: Discover the Secret to Getting Through to Absolutely Anyone* (New York: HarperCollins, 2015).

15   "Albert Mehrabian," British Library, bl.uk/people/albert-mehrabian.

16   Terry Connolly and Lars Åberg, "Some Contagion Models of Speeding," *Accident Analysis and Prevention* 25, no. 1 (1993): 57–66, doi.org/10.1016/0001-4575(93)90096-F.

17 Andrew Westbrook and Todd S. Braver, "Dopamine Does Double
Duty in Motivating Cognitive Effort," *Neuron* 89, no. 4 (2016):
695–710, doi.org/10.1016/j.neuron.2015.12.029.

18 Brenda Goodman, "Insatiable: Hedonic Hunger and the Science of
Why We Can't Stop Eating," WebMD, March 3, 2021, webmd.com/
diet/story/hedonic-hunger-and-why-we-cant-stop-eating.

19 Dennis Tirch, Benjamin Schoendorff, and Laura R. Silberstein,
*The ACT Practitioner's Guide to the Science of Compassion: Tools for
Fostering Psychological Flexibility* (Oakland, CA: New Harbinger,
2014).

20 Firdaus S. Dhabhar, "A Hassle a Day May Keep the Pathogens
Away: The Fight-or-Flight Stress Response and the Augmentation
of Immune Function," *Integrative and Comparative Biology* 49, no. 3
(2009): 215–36, doi.org/10.1093/icb/icp045.

21 Robert Ader, ed., *Psychoneuroimmunology*, 4th ed. (San Diego, CA:
Academic Press, 2006).

22 Abigail Rolston and Elizabeth Lloyd-Richardson, "What Is
Emotional Regulation and How Do We Do It?" Cornell Research
Program on Self-Injury and Recovery, n.d., selfinjury.bctr.cornell.
edu/perch/resources/what-is-emotion-regulationsinfo-brief.pdf.

23 Katharina Star, "Negative Thinking Patterns and Your Beliefs,"
Verywell Mind, October 11, 2020, verywellmind.com/
negative-thinking-patterns-and-beliefs-2584084.

24 Cristina M. Alberini, "Long-Term Memories: The Good, the Bad,
and the Ugly," *Cerebrum* 21 (2010), ncbi.nlm.nih.gov/pmc/articles/
PMC3574792.

25 Kendra Cherry, "What Is the Negativity Bias?" Verywell Mind,
April 29, 2020, verywellmind.com/negative-bias-4589618.

26 Lou Whitaker, "How Does Thinking Positive Thoughts Affect
Neuroplasticity?" Meteor Education, meteoreducation.com/
how-does-thinking-positive-thoughts-affect-neuroplasticity.

27 Joyce Shaffer, "Neuroplasticity and Clinical Practice: Building
Brain Power for Health," *Frontiers in Psychology* 7 (2016): 1118, doi.
org/10.3389/fpsyg.2016.01118.

28 Susan Reynolds, "Happy Brain, Happy Life," *Psychology
Today*, August 2, 2011, psychologytoday.com/ca/blog/
prime-your-gray-cells/201108/happy-brain-happy-life.

29 Daniel Goleman, *Focus: The Hidden Driver of Excellence* (New York:
HarperCollins, 2013).

30 Joshua O. Goh and Denise C. Park, "Neuroplasticity and Cognitive Aging: The Scaffolding Theory of Aging and Cognition," *Restorative Neurology and Neuroscience* 27, no. 5 (2009): 391–403, doi. org/10.3233/RNN-2009-0493.

31 Caroline White, "Brain Circuitry Model for Mental Illness Will Transform Management, NIH Mental Health Director Says," *BMJ* (2011): 343, doi.org/10.1136/bmj.d5581.

Chapter 8: Locking Down Your Life Course

1 Howatt, *The Cure for Loneliness*.

Chapter 9: Designing Your Life Course

1 Jodi L. Berg, "The Role of Personal Purpose and Personal Goals in Symbiotic Visions," *Frontiers in Psychology* 6 (2015): 443, doi. org/10.3389/fpsyg.2015.00443.

2 Leslie Riopel, "The Importance, Benefits, and Value of Goal Setting," Positive Psychology, June 14, 2019, positivepsychology. com/benefits-goal-setting.

Chapter 10: Showing Up as the Person You Want to Be

1 *Merriam-Webster*, s.v. "reputation (*n.*)," merriam-webster.com/ dictionary/reputation.

2 Caroline Castrillon, "Why Personal Branding Is More Important than Ever," *Forbes*, February 12, 2019, forbes.com/sites/carolinecastrillon/2019/02/12/ why-personal-branding-is-more-important-than-ever.

Chapter 11: Emotions Matter

1 Oji Emotions Life Lab, ojilifelab.com.

2 Oji Emotions Life Lab.

3 Lawrence W. Reed, "Norman Vincent Peale's Timeless Advice: Take Charge of Your Own Life, First," FEE Stories, March 23, 2020, fee.org/articles/norman-vincent-peale-s-timeless-advice-take-charge-of-your-own-life-first.

4 Adam Grant, "There's a Name for the Blah You're Feeling: It's Called Languishing," *New York Times*, April 19, 2021, nytimes.com/ 2021/04/19/well/mind/covid-mental-health-languishing.html.

5   "Chris Voss," Black Swan Group, blackswanltd.com/our-team/
    chris-voss.
6   "Emotional Dysregulation," Psychological Care and Healing Center,
    pchtreatment.com/who-we-treat/emotional-dysregulation.
7   Marc Brackett, *Managing Emotions in Times of
    Uncertainty and Stress*, Coursera, coursera.org/learn/
    managing-emotions-uncertainty-stress.

Chapter 12: Initiating Emotions

1   Kendra Cherry, "What Is Toxic Positivity?" Verywell Mind,
    verywellmind.com/what-is-toxic-positivity-5093958.
2   Allie Volpe, "'Tragic Optimism': The Antidote to Toxic
    Positivity," BBC Worklife, March 8, 2021, bbc.com/worklife/
    article/20210302-tragic-optimism-the-antidote-to-toxic-positivity.
3   Kelly Miller, "Is Happiness Genetic and What Causes It?" Positive
    Psychology, positivepsychology.com/is-happiness-genetic.
4   Arthur C. Brooks, "The 3 Equations for a Happy
    Life, Even During a Pandemic," *Atlantic*, April 9,
    2020, theatlantic.com/family/archive/2020/04/
    how-increase-happiness-according-research/609619.

Chapter 13: Think Good Thoughts

1   Christina Gregory, "The Five Stages of Grief: An Examination
    of the Kübler-Ross Model," Psycom, May 4, 2021, psycom.net/
    depression.central.grief.html.
2   King's College London, "Do Negative Thoughts Increase Risk
    of Alzheimer's Disease?" Medical Xpress, November 17, 2014,
    medicalxpress.com/news/2014-11-negative-thoughts-alzheimer-
    disease.html.
3   American Academy of Neurology, "Cynical? You May Be Hurting
    Your Brain Health," ScienceDaily, May 28, 2014, sciencedaily.com/
    releases/2014/05/140528163739.htm.
4   Christian Keysers and Valeria Gazzola, "Hebbian Learning and
    Predictive Mirror Neurons for Actions, Sensations, and Emotions,"
    Philosophical Transactions of the Royal Society B: Biological Sciences
    369, no. 1644 (2014): 20130175, doi.org/10.1098/rstb.2013.0175.
5   "Building Your Resilience," American Psychological Association,
    January 1, 2012, apa.org/topics/resilience.
6   "The Four Agreements," MiguelRuiz.com, miguelruiz.com/
    the-four-agreements.

7 Rongxiang Tang, Karl J. Friston, and Yi-Yuan Tang, "Brief
   Mindfulness Meditation Induces Gray Matter Changes
   in a Brain Hub," *Neural Plasticity* (2020): 8830005,
   doi.org/10.1155/2020/8830005.
8 Rick Hanson, "Rewire Your Brain for Lasting Well-Being
   and Inner Strength," Happify Daily, happify.com/hd/
   rewire-your-brain-for-lasting-wellbeing-and-inner-strength.
9 Jon Kabat-Zinn, "A Guide to Mindfulness," *Jon Kabat-Zinn
   Teaches Mindfulness and Meditation*, Masterclass, masterclass.com/
   classes/jon-kabat-zinn-teaches-mindfulness-and-meditation/
   chapters/a-guide-to-mindfulness.

Chapter 15: Preparing Your Mind to Be Positive

1 Susan Krauss Whitbourne, "Make Your Self-Talk Work for You,"
   Psychology Today, September 10, 2013, psychologytoday.com/ca/
   blog/fulfillment-any-age/201309/make-your-self-talk-work-you.
2 Steven G. Rogelberg et al., "The Executive Mind: Leader Self-Talk,
   Effectiveness, and Strain," *Journal of Managerial Psychology* 28, no.
   2 (2013): 183–201, doi.org/10.1108/02683941311300702.
3 "Confirmation Bias," ScienceDaily, sciencedaily.com/terms/
   confirmation_bias.htm.
4 Melanie Bauer, "How to Avoid the Temptations of Immediate
   Gratification," *Scientific American*, January 15, 2013,
   scientificamerican.com/article/how-to-avoid-the-temptations-
   of-immediate-gratification.
5 Tyler W. Watts, Greg J. Duncan, and Haonan Quan,
   "Revisiting the Marshmallow Test: A Conceptual Replication
   Investigating Links between Early Delay of Gratification
   and Later Outcomes," *Psychological Science* 29, no. 7 (2018):
   1159–77, doi.org/10.1177/0956797618761661.
6 "Patience: Don't Let Frustration Get the Better of You," Mind Tools,
   mindtools.com/pages/article/newTCS_78.htm.
7 Sarah A. Schnitker, "An Examination of Patience and Well-Being,"
   Journal of Positive Psychology 7, no. 4 (2012): 263–80, doi.org/
   10.1080/17439760.2012.697185.
8 Deb Muoio, "The Optimistic vs. the Pessimistic Employee,"
   Arch Profile, March 8, 2016, blog.archprofile.com/archinsights/
   optimistic_pessimistic.

9   Bill Taylor, "Why the Future Belongs to Tough-Minded Optimists,"
    Harvard Business Review, March 3, 2016, hbr.org/2016/03/
    why-the-future-belongs-to-tough-minded-optimists.

10 Simon Sinek, "The One with Brené Brown," *A Bit of Optimism*
    (podcast), April 13, 2021, youtube.com/watch?v=J16Zyknu9Mw.

Chapter 16: Wiring a Positive Mindset

1   Phillippa Lally et al., "How Are Habits Formed: Modelling Habit
    Formation in the Real World," *European Journal of Social Psychology*
    40, no. 6 (2010): 998–1009, doi.org/10.1002/ejsp.674.

2   James Clear, *Atomic Habits* (New York: Penguin, 2018).

3   Michael Craig Miller, "In Praise of Gratitude," Harvard Health
    Publishing, Harvard Medical School, November 21, 2012, health.
    harvard.edu/blog/in-praise-of-gratitude-201211215561.

4   Bill Howatt, "How to Keep Workers from Mentally Checking
    Out," *Globe and Mail*, September 10, 2013, theglobeandmail.
    com/report-on-business/careers/careers-leadership/
    how-to-keep-workers-from-mentally-moving-on/article14224187.

5   Amy Morin, "7 Scientifically Proven Benefits of Gratitude That
    Will Motivate You to Give Thanks Year-Round," *Forbes*, November
    23, 2014, forbes.com/sites/amymorin/2014/11/23/7-scientifically-
    proven-benefits-of-gratitude-that-will-motivate-you-to-give-thanks-
    year-round.

6   Douglas Main, "5 Scientifically Proven Benefits of Gratitude,"
    Newsweek, November 25, 2015, newsweek.com/5-scientifically-
    proven-benefits-gratitude-398582.

7   Stephanie Nicola, "How to Foster Gratitude," WebMD, August 24,
    2021, webmd.com/women/features/gratitute-health-boost.

Chapter 17: Tackling Stress and Self-Deception

1   Lori Waite Turner et al., *Life Choices: Health Concepts and Strategies*,
    2nd ed. (New York: West Publishing Company, 1992).

2   Paul M. Insel and Walton T. Roth, *Core Concepts in Health* (London:
    Mayfield Publishing Company, 2007).

3   Matthew Hutson, "Living a Lie: We Deceive Ourselves
    to Better Deceive Others," *Scientific American*,
    April 4, 2017, scientificamerican.com/article/
    living-a-lie-we-deceive-ourselves-to-better-deceive-others.

4   J.T. O'Donnell, "85 Percent of Job Applicants Lie on Resumes. Here's How to Spot a Dishonest Candidate," *Inc.*, August 15, 2017, inc.com/jt-odonnell/staggering-85-of-job-applicants-lying-on-resumes-.html.

5   Eddie Harmon-Jones and Judson Mills, "An Introduction to Cognitive Dissonance Theory and an Overview of Current Perspectives on the Theory," in *Cognitive Dissonance: Reexamining a Pivotal Theory in Psychology*, 2nd ed., Eddie Harmon-Jones, ed. (Washington, DC: American Psychological Association, 2019): 3–24, apa.org/pubs/books/Cognitive-Dissonance-Intro-Sample.pdf.

Chapter 18: Confronting a Mind Trick

1   "Does Depression Increase the Risk of Suicide?" US Department of Health and Human Services, September 16, 2014, hhs.gov/answers/mental-health-and-substance-abuse/does-depression-increase-risk-of-suicide/index.html.

2   Ramesh Shivani, R. Jeffrey Goldsmith, and Robert M. Anthenelli, "Alcoholism and Psychiatric Disorders: Diagnostic Challenges," *Alcohol Research and Health* 26, no. 2 (2002): 90–98, ncbi.nlm.nih.gov/pmc/articles/PMC6683829.

Chapter 19: Prepare–Plan–Practise

1   Bill Howatt, *The Coping Crisis: Discover Why Coping Skills Are Required for a Healthy and Fulfilling Life* (Toronto: Morneau Shepell, 2015).

2   Daniel Kahneman and Amos Tversky, "Prospect Theory: An Analysis of Decision under Risk," *Econometrica* 47, no. 2 (1979): 263–92, doi.org/10.2307/1914185.

3   "Prospect Theory," BehavioralEconomics.com, behavioraleconomics.com/resources/mini-encyclopedia-of-be/prospect-theory.

4   Susan David and Christina Congleton, "Emotional Agility," *Harvard Business Review*, November 2013, hbr.org/2013/11/emotional-agility.

5   Fahimeh Kashani et al., "Effect of Stress Inoculation Training on the Levels of Stress, Anxiety, and Depression in Cancer Patients," *Iranian Journal of Nursing and Midwifery Research* 20, no. 3 (2015): 359–64, ncbi.nlm.nih.gov/pmc/articles/PMC4462062.

Appendix B: Happiness IQ Quick Screen

1   Esteban Ortiz-Ospina and Max Roser, "Happiness and Life
Satisfaction," Our World in Data, 2013, ourworldindata.org/
happiness-and-life-satisfaction.

2   "Ed Diener," Pursuit of Happiness, pursuit-of-happiness.org/
history-of-happiness/ed-diener.

3   Belle Beth Cooper, "10 Simple Things You Can Do Today that will
Make You Happier, Backed by Science," *Buffer blog*, April 28, 2018,
buffer.com/resources/be-happy-today.

Appendix C: Optimism Quick Screen

1   "Can Optimism Make a Difference in Your Life?"
Health Encyclopedia, University of Rochester Medical
Center, urmc.rochester.edu/encyclopedia/content.
aspx?ContentTypeID=1&ContentID=4511.

Index

About the Author

FOUNDER OF Howatt HR and known internationally as one of Canada's top experts in workplace mental health, Dr. Bill Howatt has thirty-plus years of experience in mental health and addictions counselling, HR, and leadership. He is active in workplace mental health research, chair of CSA Z1008: Management of Impairment in the Workplace, and creator of the University of New Brunswick's Certificate in Psychologically Safe Leadership, and he has published over five hundred articles and fifty books.

Other books in the Break Through series by Dr. Bill Howatt:

Stop Hiding and Start Living
How to Say F-it to Fear and
Develop Mental Fitness

The Cure for Loneliness
How to Feel Connected and
Escape Isolation

Thinking about Mental Fitness is Much Harder Than Doing It.

ARE YOU CONCERNED about your workers' stress, risk of burnout, or mental health?

To hire Dr. Bill Howatt to speak with your team or at your event, visit **billhowatt.com**.

Continue the conversation by following Bill on social media:
🐦 **twitter.com/billhowatt**
in **linkedin.com/in/howatthr**

Thank you for reading this book and working on your journey through languishing. My own life has not been an easy path, and I understand the daily struggle of being a human being. But there is a path to mental fitness, and you are on it!

BILL HOWATT